Rails&
Rooms

A Timeless Canadian Journey

Rails&
Rooms

A Timeless Canadian Journey

Dave Preston

Whitecap
Toronto/Vancouver

Edited by Elaine Jones
Proofread by Elizabeth Salomons
Cover design by Maxine Lea
Interior design by Warren Clark

Printed in Canada

National Library of Canada Cataloguing in Publication Data
Preston, Dave 1956–
Rails and rooms

Includes index
ISBN 1-55285-009-9

1. Preston, Dave 1956—Journeys—Canada 2. Canada—Description and travel. 3. Railroad travel—Canada. 4. Hotels—Canada. 5. Railroad travel—Canada—History I. Title
FC75.P73 2001   917.104'648   C2001-910532-0
F1017.P73 2001

The publisher acknowledges the support of the Canada Council for the Arts for our publishing program and the Cultural Services Branch of the Government of British Columbia in making this publication possible. We acknowledge the financial support of the Government of Canada through the Book Publishing Industry Development Program for our publishing activities

For more information on other titles from Whitecap Books, visit our web site at www.whitecap.ca

This book is dedicated
to the men and women
who built, ran and continue to run
Canadian railways.

Contents

Acknowledgements

THE JOURNEY I MADE WOULD NOT HAVE BEEN POSSIBLE WITHOUT THE tremendous support of many people and companies. I thank each and every one of them.

Malcolm Andrews, Trianda Barton and all the staff of VIA Rail.

Deena Fisher Abadiano, Karina Davies, Laura Fairweather, Trudy Fitzgerald, Samantha Geer, Sean Guthrie, Nancie Hall, Jill Killeen, Ann Layton, Deneen Perrin, Karen Reichendaugh, Nathalie Samson, Tom Smith, Andrew Turnbull, Serena Veevers, Holly Wood, David Woodward and the staff of CP (& Fairmont) Hotels.

Sherraine Christopherson and the Fort Garry Hotel.

Michele Facey and Delta Hotels.

George MacPherson and Hertz Canada Ltd.

The B.C. Ferry Corporation.

Nancy Williatte-Battet, Robert C Kennell, Jo-Anne Colby and the CP Archives.

Susan Kooymar and the Glenbow Archives.

Peggy Amirault, Lorraine Buchanan, José Castineiras, Elaine Jones, Marie Hansen, Hélèna Katz, Barbara King, David C. Knowles, Clare Mackay, Julia Matusky, Judy Patt, Doreen Pendgracs, Myrna Proulx, John and Carol Rowling, Gary D. Shutlak, Suzanne Steele. Special thanks to Robin Rivers for her patience and support.

And, of course, huge thanks to the Preston girls — Lesley, Jenn and Debbie.

Introduction

THERE ARE MANY WAYS TO GET FROM A TO B — OR FROM HALIFAX, Nova Scotia, to Victoria, British Columbia, for that matter. I've flown this expanse, driven most of it, ridden a motorcycle across much of it, and hiked for days along its lakesides and riverbanks. But it wasn't until I rode a train for 4,414 miles across every Canadian province that still has a track that I truly appreciated this country's size and diversity.

Our nation's love of rail travel has been a torrid and well-documented affair, spanning more than a century and a half. Canadian railway history can be traced through hundreds of separate companies to its birth in 1836, when the Champlain & St. Lawrence Railroad became the first public railway in the land. In 1850, Upper Canada had just sixty-six miles of railway track, but by 1943 there were more than 43,000 miles of route being operated by thirty-eight separate corporations. Between 1900 and 1916, railway mileage in Canada increased from 17,000 miles to more than 40,000. (Incidentally, you may wonder about the use of imperial measurement in this book. Railways were built mile by mile, today's locomotives still show the driver speeds in miles per hour, and white mile markers picket their way along every rail corridor still in use — using imperial seems to make the most sense.)

In 1944, thanks to gas rationing and the movement of troops, Canadian railways carried 44 million passengers. The following year, more than 63 billion ton-miles of freight were moved by rail. The Canadian National Railway (CNR) alone had 21,000 miles of track at that point, making it the world's largest railway system operating under one management (unless we include the lines run under various managements across the USSR). Meanwhile, the Canadian Pacific Railway (CPR) was the largest privately owned rail system in the world and can arguably lay claim to being the founder of Canadian tourism. For a while the cheapest and, oddly enough, the most efficient means of getting from Europe to the Far East was to take weeks or months to cross the country by train, then board a steamship on the west coast. The men and women of the Canadian railways made sure the train trip was an enjoyable experience (and a profitable one for the railways).

Though I certainly wasn't heading to the Orient, the romance of travelling this country's breadth from east to west by train had captured my imagination. I was lured much as those before me had been, but perhaps not by the same sales pitch. An 1887 CPR brochure titled *The New Highway to the East Across the Mountains, Prairies and Rivers of Canada* dangled a most exotic carrot for the would-be passenger:

> May I not tempt you, kind reader, to leave England for a few short weeks and journey with me across that broad land, the beauties and glories of which have only now been brought within our reach? There will be no hardships to endure, no difficulties to overcome, and no dangers or annoyances whatever. You shall see mighty rivers, vast forests, boundless plains, stupendous mountains and wonders innumerable; and you shall see all in comfort, nay, in luxury. If you are a jaded tourist, sick of Old World scenes and smells, you will find everything here fresh and novel. If you are a sportsman, you will meet with unlimited opportunities and endless variety, and no one shall deny your right to hunt or fish at your own sweet will. If you are a mountain climber, you shall have cliffs and peaks and glaciers worthy of your alpenstock, and if you have lived

in India, and tiger hunting has lost its zest, a Rocky Mountain grizzly bear will renew your interest in life.

Tiger hunting had never had any zest for me, but I wanted to see Canada from a passenger train window, in real time. I wanted to head west from one bordering ocean to the other, at a speed that would make changes in topography barely perceivable. But then, as hours rolled into days, I'd appreciate the grand geographical and cultural differences that both separate and unite our regions. A train, I thought, would provide a journey that would get me right *into* Canada, tunnelling through rock when it had to.

In his 1934 book, *English Journey,* British author J.B. Priestley wrote:

> When people moved slowly in their travel there was time to establish proper communications with what was strange, to absorb, to adjust oneself. Now that we are whizzed about the world, there is no time for absorbing and adjusting. Perhaps it is for this reason that the world that the traveller knows is beginning to show less and less variety. By the time we can travel at four hundred miles an hour we shall probably move over a dead uniformity, so that the bit of reality we left at one end of a journey is twin to the bit of reality we step into at the other end. Indeed, by that time there will be movement, but, strictly speaking, no more travel.

I wanted to experience the many realities of Canada and enjoy the hospitality that each region could offer. I was also aware that our love affair with rail travel, as much as it still glows warmly and feeds on the fuel of nostalgia, might be a fleeting thing. Subsidized passenger trains threading their way across this land are not to be taken for granted.

Upon completing Canada's first transcontinental railroad, the grandfather of CPR, William Cornelius Van Horne, said: "If we can't export the scenery, we'll import the tourists." By 1900, the CPR had thriving hotels in Montreal, Quebec City, Banff, Lake Louise and Vancouver. At first these hotels were not the world-famous destinations they are for today's tourists; more often they were simply comfortable stopping-off points for those affluent travellers en route to the Orient.

Our trains, thank God and many a taxpayer, still live. We've spent more than a century proving there's a cheaper, faster way to get anywhere. But it's not always a better way, and people are still riding trains.

In 1977, the passenger services of both CN and Canadian Pacific were entrusted to a new Crown corporation, VIA Rail. After more than seventy-five years as a government-owned railway, Canadian National was privatized in 1995 and continues to carry huge volumes of freight. CP is an international multi-billion-dollar enterprise, with more corporate operations than most of us would care to count.

Like the railways that bore and nurtured them, the Canadian railway hotels spin a story that is long and perplexing, involving all manner of politics, confounding economics, hundreds of companies and thousands of business deals. (During the course of writing this book another change took place, one that sees some of the hotel names being prefixed with the word Fairmont. However, in the interests of tradition and simplicity, I have used the hotel name that is familiar to most people.) My story doesn't simplify or explain this complex evolution; it is merely a personal account of a train journey that includes visits to some of the grand hotels that still provide rest and relaxation for travellers. This is the story of a month-long trip that took me gently across Canada, and occasionally through time.

Halifax

~*to*~
Moncton

Fog. It's what I expected, descending through dense cloud onto the wet runway at Halifax airport a little before 7 a.m. Fog, or mist if you prefer a more romantic word, is what most Canadians expect of the Atlantic coast. Typical Maritimes weather I thought, as I pulled my jacket out of the overhead luggage compartment and pushed my arms into it. Cool and foggy. When I got off the plane, though, the humidity and heat surprised me. It was typical for early September, according to Peggy, the friend who met me and drove me the half-hour or so to the downtown core.

I suggested I pay for the ride by buying breakfast, and being a local she suggested the Ardmore Tea Room. Named for a Lord Ardmore who once owned a sizable chunk of the town, and run by Tennyson Cormier and his wife, Norma, this small culinary fixture of Halifax opened just before I was born. Having gone without sleep for some thirty-odd hours, a huge plate of salt cod fish cakes, fried eggs and toast was not exactly what I had in mind. However, I was determined to get this journey off on the right foot by accepting whatever local hospitality was offered. I'm pleased I did.

With a pot of industrial-strength tea, this first meal set me up nicely for a month or so away from home comforts, and all for just a few dollars. Served with home-style hospitality amid chattering neighbourhood regulars, it proved to be a very warm welcome. The place has barely changed since the

1950s, and its popularity with locals may be due to the fact that tourists don't often find it and probably wouldn't be impressed by the architecture or the interior decor if they did.

Halifax is a good place to begin a cross-country railway journey. Millions have done it before me and Nova Scotia pops up in many railway history books. In 1720, horses pulled supplies on a short tramway to the French fortress at Louisbourg, then in 1818 a similar tramway hauled coal at Pictou. A regular rail track was laid eleven years later, using the first metal rails used in Canada, possibly in North America. In 1830 the Sydney Mines Railway opened, as did the two-mile Bridgeport Tramway. All told, the Maritimers were among the first Canadians on track for rail travel and apart from that, Halifax is about the farthest east I can climb aboard for such a trip. In 1988, CN abandoned the last part of the railway in Newfoundland, and on New Year's Eve, 1989, Prince Edward Island lost its rail service.

Breakfast over and back into the steamy heat of the morning, I begged a lift to the hotel I'd booked into, just across from the downtown waterfront. The Delta Halifax, which used to be the Canadian Pacific's Chateau Halifax, sits grey and squarely opposite docks No. 10 and 11, tucked behind a raised section of highway in the Scotia Square complex. It's built on the site of a Chinese laundry and whorehouse but sailors come and go, or at least came and went, and times have changed. From my respectable fourth-floor room looking to the east I saw part of the star-shaped Citadel up the hill to my right, and the Department of National Defence fuel docks over in Dartmouth across to my left. There was more to see, and I aimed to see it, but the fish cakes and me were in need of immediate, serious sleep.

After my nap, the hotel's retired assistant manager, José Castineiras, took me for lunch in a quiet back corner of the hotel dining room. Over bowls of wholesome chowder, pan-fried halibut and roasted Yukon Gold potatoes, he told me how the hotel hit its peak in the 1970s. It was *the* place to go

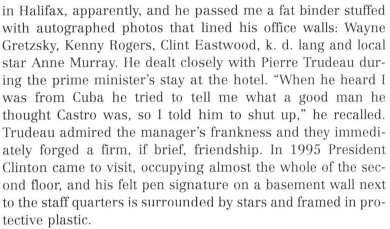

in Halifax, apparently, and he passed me a fat binder stuffed with autographed photos that lined his office walls: Wayne Gretzsky, Kenny Rogers, Clint Eastwood, k. d. lang and local star Anne Murray. He dealt closely with Pierre Trudeau during the prime minister's stay at the hotel. "When he heard I was from Cuba he tried to tell me what a good man he thought Castro was, so I told him to shut up," he recalled. Trudeau admired the manager's frankness and they immediately forged a firm, if brief, friendship. In 1995 President Clinton came to visit, occupying almost the whole of the second floor, and his felt pen signature on a basement wall next to the staff quarters is surrounded by stars and framed in protective plastic.

José, justly proud of the fame and business he helped to bring to the hotel with his gala banquets and themed promotions, such as Mexican Night, is one of those people who do not go gentle into that good retirement. He regaled me for hours with tales of ejecting she-males from washrooms, arresting guests who were "borrowing" TV sets or stuffing their luggage with CP's trademark orange towels. Popular with the theatre crowd, the hotel's Dick Turpin pub was so busy during the 1970s that waitresses bribed the cooks with pitchers of beer to get their orders out on time. Success continued through to the 1990s, bringing the hotel more than a million dollars a year in profits.

We adjourned downstairs to Sam Slick's Bar, named for a character created by Thomas Haliburton, a Nova Scotia judge. Slick stood "as large as life and twice as natural," and his bar was a comfortable place to sit and sip with an eye on the time, since the walls were hung with dozens of clocks. José ended the session with an account of what must surely be a record in the hotel industry. Former prime minister Joe Clark and his wife were scheduled to check in to the hotel at 4 p.m. At one o'clock the ceiling of the reserved room collapsed, showering everything with a dusty white mess. José immediately sent one employee out to Eaton's to buy carpeting, and another to a paint store. Within three hours they completely replastered and painted the room and fitted the new broadloom.

Perhaps the talk of how much could be accomplished in three hours reminded me how little I'd done in six, so after a fond farewell I set out to explore the town.

The immediate neighbourhood is one of those modern affairs designed more for tires than feet. I clambered over a concrete barrier or two, scampered between speeding vehicles and soon found myself on a cement walkway outside the waterfront casino, as big and grey as the sky above. I wasn't sure what I'd find in Halifax or what I was looking for, but this wasn't it. Across a short stretch of water, though, I spied my first piece of legend: Halifax Pier. Apart from being the final resting place for one of Barrett's Privateers, courtesy of troubadour Stan Rogers, this is also where the schooner from the backside of a Canadian dime lives. Sadly, the famous *Bluenose II* was away at sea and tied up in its place was a nondescript boat.

I wandered the narrow old streets of the pier district, now loud and heavy with tourists, attracted to gift shops and cafés like the Privateer's Warehouse and the Old Red Store. I succumbed and bought what I always buy when I'm at the seaside, an ice cream cone, and then I watched the oldest continuous-running saltwater ferry in North America ply its way between Halifax and Dartmouth, about a mile away.

Way off to my left, farther into the harbour somewhere, sat Pier Number 1, where the "Death Ship" *Mackay-Bennett* docked in April, 1912, carrying victims of the Titanic. Halifax enjoyed, if that's the right word, a lot of tourist attention after Hollywood's coverage of that infamous maritime disaster. Not being one to ignore such hype, I went along to the Maritime Museum of the Atlantic, suitably installed on Lower Water Street, to see the *Titanic* exhibits. Void of movie glitz and uncluttered by pretty people, the surviving artifacts told a sorrowful tale. I was also moved by the exhibits that recounted the Halifax Explosion of 1917, a tragic event that killed two thousand people and injured a further nine thousand. A French munitions ship, *Mont Blanc,* had arrived in port that

December to join a convoy when it collided with another vessel, the steamship *Imo*. After fire broke out, the crews jumped ship and swam for the shore. The explosion demolished the entire north end of Halifax, and many survivors made a temporary home in the citadel. A downtown church withstood the blast, but a broken window in the building remains, the profile of an unfortunate face blown into it. By necessity, Halifax soon learned to cope with more than the average population of blind and disabled citizens.

I left the museum and stumbled upon a wild bunch of Acadians, descendants of those first French-American pioneers, hell-bent on having a festival in the parking lot, doing things that probably led to them being expelled from here by the British in 1755. Needless to say, I was soon waving a red, white and blue tricolour, complete with yellow star, and caught up in a swirl of noisy step-dancing, fiddle-playing and aromatic food booths.

It was all fun and games, but I realized my stay here was short. If I was to get to the true heart of Halifax, to the essence of what makes Atlantic culture so richly appealing to the rest of Canada, I ought to follow the call of a malty siren to a good hostelry and meet the locals. Minutes later I sat in a friendly bar in the cool basement of the Granite Pub, a thick, stone building on Barrington Street, not far from the railway station. Granite brews its own beer and hand-pulls it to the glass via an authentic British beer pump. As far as I was concerned, which was as far as I could see through the bottom of a pint glass laced with beer froth, this first day had been one hell of a success. The locals blessed and toasted my pending journey. Several times.

I returned the next day to the south end of the city, to explore the train station, once connected by rails to neighbouring docks. Pier 21, a ten-minute walk from the train station, poured out thousands of immigrants and travellers from steamships. In July of 1928 alone, thirteen ships from Cunard and White Star docked here, carrying more than seven thousand passengers. Many jumped aboard a train and took off to Montreal or Quebec City, or continued west to the prairies and beyond. About a million immigrants arrived in Canada through Pier 21 between 1928 and 1971, most of them from Europe. Many rode the track to various points west. The fare from Halifax to Vancouver, a posted distance of 3,475 miles, was $23.85 in 1938, and still only $55 twenty years later.

The huge building, once drafty and noisy, is now a polished museum, and one that easily lured me in. Inside is an immigrant's-eye view of the Canadian welcome — which was quite Spartan. Hard wooden benches and fenced-in areas were their first taste of the better life they had travelled so many miles to find. The entrance interview, often conducted with help of an interpreter, asked many probing questions: Can you read? By whom was the passage paid? And my favourite question: Have you or any of your family been mentally defective? Those who passed the exam were put aboard trains to all parts of the country. According to a former immigration official I met, Italians were among those let through most quickly, thanks to the smelly meats and cheeses they stowed in their baggage.

During the Second World War, 494,874 Canadians left for Europe from Pier 21. About 45,000 lost their lives and of those who returned, 55,000 came back injured. (When VE Day was announced, military revellers got so carried away that Halifax was all but trashed in a two-day riotous party.) This building has seen a nation's share of bittersweet memories, bewildered hellos and tearful goodbyes.

Aside from housing the museum, piers 21, 20 and 22 berth cruise ships. While I was there one of the biggest in the world, a monstrous white vessel called *Carnival Triumph,* docked and let its noisy human cargo spill out to shop at market stalls set up in the old warehouse next door. I dodged past a couple of kilted pipers who were blowing a Celtic welcome and slipped away to the peace of the old railway station.

The VIA Rail Station in Halifax stands near the foot of Hollis Street, a short block from the waterfront and across the road from a small park named in honour of Edward Cornwallis, the man who claims to have got here first in 1749. A monument dedicated to the early Ukrainian settlers, so many of whom first stepped on Canadian soil here, stands proudly in the park's centre. The station is simply one rectangular hall flanked by a few small offices and stores. It looks robust and handsome, built of stone quarried in New Brunswick and brought here by rail cars in the 1920s.

Bedecked with coloured flags and plants, it's a cheerful enough place to wait for a train, and there's only one a day. I took out my camera and had barely snapped the first picture when a short, stocky man came up and showed more than casual interest. Bill Mont introduced himself with a firm handshake. He'd worked on the railway for many years and now ran a small auctioneering and flea market business from an office in the station.

The main hall of Halifax Station is now available for private functions, between trains, of course. Photo: Dave Preston

His career began in 1941 when he was thirteen years old and spent his days picking up trash from around the station. Promotion to washroom-cleaning duties came soon after and before long he was a fully fledged redcap, hauling luggage for immigrants and tourists to and from the platform. He helped movie stars such as Alan Ladd disembark at Pier 21 and board trains heading to various cities in Quebec and Ontario.

After the war, thanks to a system of centralized transport, Halifax was a major port with a busy railway hub and upwards of eighty trains a day came and went along the old Intercolonial line, now run by CNR. The passenger trains often filled the lengthy platforms here with almost twenty cars. Bill has watched the decline of the railway system with sadness.

I noticed an old man in a green shirt and plaid pants wandering around the station, fishing pop bottles and cans out of the garbage bins. Bill saw me watching. "That's Harold Travis," he said. "He was stationmaster here for forty-odd years." Bill took me by the arm and pulled me over to meet him and we sat down together at one of the tables. Harold can't speak too well since suffering a stroke, but the bright blue eyes behind his gold-rimmed glasses make it clear he hears every question, and he's eager to answer. His mouth, beneath a neat, white mustache, twitches in frustration, but I can't decipher the sounds coming out of it. I soon realize that questions with numerical answers are easiest, so I ask when he started working here. His pale finger draws an invisible 1940 on the white tabletop between us. How many years did you work here? The finger draws fifty-one. His age, according to the finger, is seventy-five.

Harold was also in charge of the newsies, a long-gone breed of guys who boarded the train with a crate of newspapers and assorted items to sell to passengers. As a favour, Bill once worked a shift with a newsie. "It was horrendous. I was staggering through each carriage saying, 'Need a paper, wanna buy a deck o' cards?' Hardest job I ever did."

These days the railway station sees long periods of quiet,

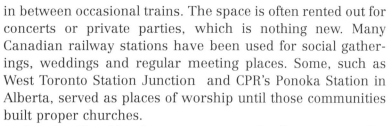

in between occasional trains. The space is often rented out for concerts or private parties, which is nothing new. Many Canadian railway stations have been used for social gatherings, weddings and regular meeting places. Some, such as West Toronto Station Junction and CPR's Ponoka Station in Alberta, served as places of worship until those communities built proper churches.

Leaving Harold to hunt pop cans and Bill to organize his flea markets, I found the door connecting the station, via a short passageway, to the Nova Scotian, the railway hotel that opened next door in 1930.

For many years, the Nova Scotian was the only CN hotel that was profitable on a year-round basis. The navy brought lots of trade, but that's dropped off lately, replaced by business people and convention crowds.

Until the late 1970s, hotel staff did all the laundry for the trains, which amounted to four times the volume done for today's guests. The days when these large kitchens were kept busy providing food for railway passengers and the dining cars are gone, though the hotel still provides the train with a few supplies.

A covered walkway from Pier 21 led steamship passengers right to the Nova Scotian's door (and led many bridegrooms away to war in Europe after spending their honeymoon night at the hotel). The station has just a small café, so passengers looking for a more substantial meal visit the Promenade Lounge on the hotel's ground floor. I did just that and met Roy, a Halifax native and bartender here for close to forty years.

Roy can mix all kinds of cocktails and learned recipes for 150 while doing his six weeks' bartender training in the summer of 1963. His Caesar remains the most popular, but he poured me a pint of delicious brown ale from a local outfit, Garrison Brewing, and we talked. Conversation comes easily to Roy.

"Lots of people used to arrive here by rail," he said, "but not any more. The station had no bar of its own, and it was a big barn of a building, so during the sixties everyone came into the hotel for a drink, especially returning sailors."

That evening the bar was fairly quiet, but the hotel still accommodates some VIA rail staff and a few airline employees. Roy said Halifax is a tourist destination, with lots of U.S. visitors who come to take pictures of Peggy's Cove, just forty-five minutes down the road, or head off in boats to steal a photo of a whale.

Roy told me of guests who expired while in residence, though I'm not supposed to write about it. I asked if the place was haunted and he mentioned something about the fifth floor, but then suddenly remembered he wasn't supposed to say things like that. Ghost stories are the bane of the hotel industry. For every guest who wants to walk the hallway or sleep in the room where the headless spectre appeared, there'll be another dozen who'll avoid the place like the plague and settle for a modern and spiritually clean motel. Ghosts, generally, are not as good for hotels as, say, movie stars or famous musicians. Country star Faith Hill, for instance, stayed here when she came to surprise her man, Tim McGraw, by joining him on stage during a concert. A fashionable band of teen idols, the Backstreet Boys, took over the eleventh floor with their entourage of security personnel, but they caused no more trouble than the Duke of Windsor, who stayed there previously. The best rooms include the Crown suite on the eleventh floor with its living room, dining room, kitchen and two bedrooms, and the Vice Regal suite with similar amenities on the fifth floor.

The Lord Nelson is this city's other major railway hotel, opened on October 22, 1928, the day after Trafalgar Day. Built as a joint enterprise between eight local businessmen and the CPR, which at that point ran the Dominion Atlantic Railway, it cost $1.5 million. Montreal architect Kenneth Campbell designed it in the Georgian style with a Nova Scotia granite base, Bedford limestone and Bluenose-faced brick. Several renovations, including the addition of towers in 1967 and 1973, have somewhat wiped the original Georgian smile off the hotel's face.

The time came for me to leave Roy to shake his stainless cocktail jug for someone else, while I wandered back through town to my own modest room at the Delta Halifax. A good night's sleep was in order — I was about to make the real start of my rail journey, and that probably meant the real end of large beds.

For some odd reason, I didn't want to leave Halifax. My hotel bedsheets clung to me as a fretful mother would, but I eventually broke free, packed my bags, and checked out. Crossing the street through a thick, humid mist, I bade a quick farewell to the pier and the old part of town. Poking about between buildings and docks I made my way carefully down narrow wet steps to water level. Call me romantic, but I wanted to do what so many other trans-Canadian travellers have done before me: take a splash of the Atlantic to pour into the Pacific at my journey's end. I soon had an empty film canister filled, sealed and tucked safely into a pocket.

I caught a cab to the train station just before noon and saw another huge cruise ship, the *Norwegian Night,* dwarfing the pier buildings a couple of hundred yards away. Entering the station, I heard an announcement in English and French over the PA system, but I couldn't make out either version. The hall, as an acoustic engineer

Engineer Jim relaxes before the Halifax to Moncton run.
Photo: Dave Preston

would say, is full of active surfaces, or echoey, as the rest of us would say. I checked in two pieces of luggage for VIA train No. 15, scheduled to leave for Moncton at 1:30 p.m. With more than half an hour to spend, I sat and watched people go up to the counter to buy tickets. The travellers were a real assortment, and most seemed to be locals — some travelling light with just the clothes on their backs and others with enough luggage to rupture an elephant. I saw more than one tearful farewell, a few bilingual goodbyes and lots of hugging.

A few people stood around, unsure of their roles in this pageant. I think the only way to spend time at a train station, or a bus depot or airport, is on your own. Free of the need to make promises of writing or calling or keeping in touch, unencumbered by the guesswork of when to give that final hug, or whether to kiss on the cheek or the lips. Not worrying about whether to whisper "I love you" as you finally break away. Goodbyes are stressful, so not having to say one here in Halifax lightened my load, leaving me free to watch others leap or fall through emotional hoops.

Passengers boarding The Ocean *at Halifax will soon leave the misty shores of the Atlantic behind.* Photo: Dave Preston

I turned towards the platform doorway, just in time to be caught by my friend Peggy, who'd brought her mother along to meet me and say goodbye. I thanked them for their Halifax hospitality and made a quick dash through the hoops: firm hug, cheek kiss, promise to keep in touch. Then I strode out of the station into the pale sunlight and relative quiet of the platform.

Walking the length of the train, I took a quick inventory of what made up this first vehicle of my journey: the signature park car, with its bar lounge and upstairs dome observation room, three sleepers, a coach, a dining car, another park car, three more coaches and right behind the locomotive, as always, the baggage car.

When I finally got to the front, past big yellow locomotives No. 6432 and 6458, I saw the engineer taking a break. His name was Jim and he was sitting on the side of the track. He said it was "too bloody hot" to get in the cab just yet, so I sat down next to him and we chatted. A railroader for twenty-seven years, he told me how the three-thousand-horsepower diesel-electric engines would take about four and a half hours to haul us all to Moncton, at an average speed of seventy-five miles per hour, which he hoped would get some air going through his cab windows and cool things down. On a passenger train, the engineer makes sure the luggage is safely stowed in the baggage car and that the locomotives have whatever fuel they need. Meanwhile, the service crew, supervised by a service manager, looks after all the passengers and makes sure they get on board and into their allocated seats or cabins. The engineer is eventually told that all are aboard, that doors are shut, and that he can move off. It's a loose team but it works. Jim said he tended to keep to himself, but he was friendly enough with me.

Walking farther up the line to take a photo of my long rail journey's first train, I stopped to examine the railroad ties. Wooden. These things have barely changed in over a hundred years. The average Canadian railroad tie is eight feet long by eight inches wide and about six inches deep, and they're laid a foot to sixteen inches apart. I dug out a pocket calculator to do some quick math. A hundred ties equal about 166 feet, which puts about 3,168 of them in each linear mile of track. I reckoned I had to cross more than 600,000 to reach Moncton. I also reckoned that wandering about jabbing numbers into a small calculator can make you miss your train, so I jogged back more than a hundred yards, or 180 ties, to a service attendant. He helped me into car No. 8100, about halfway along the train, and I walked a few steps down the aisle to find my seat.

The carriage was uncrowded and comfortable, with lots of room to spread my stuff on adjacent seats or stow it on the baggage rack above me. It wasn't at all like the inaugural train of these parts. One bright May morning in 1875 more than a thousand excited people were crammed like cattle into open cars for the Western Counties Railway's first run from Yarmouth to Pitman's. Having organized the Intercolonial Railway in 1867 and assumed ownership of the railways in Nova Scotia and New Brunswick, the government of Canada soon realized these railways would never be a commercial success. They did create employment, however, and helped

establish villages and towns along the route. Canadian National's extremely busy main line would later follow much of the Inter-colonial's route.

I listened for the fabled "All aboard!" call from

A cosy room with a rolling bed and a constantly changing view. Photo: Dave Preston

VIA No. 15, The Ocean *is about to begin its 836-mile journey from Halifax to Montreal.* Photo: Dave Preston

the conductor, but, sadly, it never came. This is partly because there is no conductor these days; most of his duties went to the service manager. Bang on time, we pulled out of the station, and my trans-Canadian journey was underway. Within minutes, as we hugged the shoreline of Bedford Basin, rain streaked the windows and the sky turned the colour of an old bruise. Feeling fidgety, I wandered the length of the train, checking out the dome car and greeting those passengers whose eyes I caught. Most were heading to Montreal or Toronto, and when I said I was bound for Victoria, the conversation faltered. After all, there are planes that go there. For these people the train is still a viable means of transportation, not just some lumbering curio from a bygone era. This train, VIA No. 15, known as *The Ocean,* is the longest-running train in Canada, having operated continuously over the same 840-mile route from Halifax to Montreal since July 3, 1904. It was apparent, though, from the looks and

A VIA service manager finds office space when and where he can. Photo: Dave Preston

comments, that normal people don't use a train to get across the country.

I ended up in a vestibule between cars, talking to David, the service attendant. He told me he loved his job, and chatting to passengers and taking care of them came easily, "Though it's not a career," he said, adding that he had plans for university at some point. There's a definite sense of family about the service crew, and he referred to each of them affectionately, telling me where they were from, how long they'd been with VIA, who smoked and who didn't.

Later, while wandering towards the front of the train, I found the service manager in his office — a group of four seats he'd taken over and spread his paperwork across.

His job is largely making sure the passengers are on board, happy and have paid for their tickets. His biggest problem that day was that he had to "break the train" at some point to pick up more sleeper cars. Although summer was on the wane, tourists were still flocking to Canada and wanted to ride the rails. These cars would eventually be added to VIA's famous train No. 1, *The Canadian,* on its run from Toronto to Vancouver.

We pulled into the first station, Truro, and I jumped down onto the platform to take a photo. It was cold and wet but I was enthusiastic. By the third station, Amherst, two-thirds of the way to Moncton, the enthusiasm had waned but the downpour hadn't. I huddled into a corner of the red sandstone station and watched as the engineers unhitched the last few cars, shunted a few hundred yards up the track to pick up a few sleeper cars, then rolled back to pick up the rear end again. The whole operation took less than ten minutes, which was enough time to set me on the way to moist hypothermia. I made a small bet with myself that engineer Jim had probably had his fill of cool, fresh air and that his cab window was now closed. Yes, *this* is Maritimes weather, I told myself.

As night draws in and the scenic views disappear, the choice of seating in the rear park car improves enormously. Photo: Dave Preston

Back aboard, I found the help-yourself means to make tea in a park car, and my world slowly came pulsing back to life, though the afternoon was still grey and dark. It stayed that way as we rolled past estuaries, tidal flats, and creeks and rivers heavy with mud — known to Maritimers as guts — and on towards Moncton, where I'd spend the night. I was visiting Moncton not because of its fame as a railway hotel city, but so I could make a side trip down to St. Andrews, which does have a renowned hotel but no longer has a railroad to take me there.

Two minutes before scheduled arrival time, just as the rain stopped, we pulled into Moncton Station.

Moncton
~to~
St. Andrews

"WELCOME TO MONCTON, NEW BRUNSWICK!" I SAID TO MYSELF out loud, since no one else was there to say it as I reached the exit of the railway station. A huge parking lot that I suspected was rarely choked with vehicles surrounded me.

The bordering marshland of the Petitcodiac River, which fattens enough a few hundred yards behind the station to be called Petitcodiac Lake, was reclaimed by railway developers late last century, partly to accommodate extensive workshops and yards. A sizeable roundhouse boasting forty stalls was kept busy; the city provided repair and maintenance shops for all locomotives, passenger and freight cars for a region taking in Prince Edward Island, Nova Scotia, the whole of New Brunswick and a good chunk of eastern Quebec. That was until the 1930s. Operational headquarters of the Intercolonial Railway, the nucleus of the Canadian Government Railways, were set up in Moncton, but much administration went west, to Ottawa and Montreal.

Known as the "downtown railway lands," for obvious reasons, this expanse of almost eighty acres was redeveloped by CN in the 1960s, when it levelled the large, red brick railway station to make way for the modest building I now stood outside, as well as the parking lot, of course.

I waved to the only car in the lot, a white taxi. It whisked me down Main Street to a pair of large iron gates in a red brick wall, turned into a courtyard and stopped by the front entrance to my hotel, the Beauséjour.

Moncton was just recovering from a bout of Francophone summit meetings, and a boxy, temporary wooden structure bridged the gap between the hotel and an adjacent building. Built along Hollywood lines of architecture, best seen from one side only, the framing had served as an atrium for summit delegates. A hotel worker told me it would soon be dismantled and given to the local farmers' market.

At the check-in desk I was politely told not to drink the water as the whole city was suffering from "some biological thing." Ice, should I require any, would be "imported." As water doesn't constitute a large part of my daily intake I wasn't too worried, but I took the bottled stuff they offered me, in case I brushed my teeth or something.

I shivered myself into the fourth-floor room, cranked up the heating, and took a quick look at the view: a small clock tower a couple of blocks down Main Street, the grey and red roofs of a few neighbouring buildings, and a glimpse of the sluggish, dark green river beyond. A local attraction, according to a brochure in my room, is the tidal bore, which even merits its own little downtown park from which to witness the phenomenon. The Bay of Fundy has the biggest tides in the world, and Moncton's river water, being within tidal reach, is pushed back upstream twice a day as the ocean shoves its way inland. I promised myself I'd see this natural wonder and the next show was scheduled for ten minutes past eleven that night.

After a hot shower and a change into dry clothes I returned the thermostat to a sensible setting and wandered downstairs to the third floor, noticing a tidy little swimming pool. The still, pale blue water looked inviting but I'd been wet enough for one day. Beside the pool was a well-equipped, though lonely, workout room. I wasn't about to break its silence with my grunts and groans, so I let gravity pull me down another flight where I discovered a pleasing exhibition of Francophone visual art in a mezzanine gallery. Why they had to label visual art as Francophone I wasn't sure, but guessed it was something to do with the recent conference, or politics and government funding in general. I spent a few minutes admiring the oil paintings and sculptures, then took the stairs down to the lobby. Making my way through a raucous crowd of New Brunswick Federation of Labour conventioneers, freshly released, presumably, from a day of being locked up in meetings, I armed myself with a downtown walking map from a rack by the back door, and went out into the courtyard.

The Beauséjour forms part of a complex called Assumption Plaza, incorporating a few shops and offices. I made my way through the hallways and finished up on a wet Main Street. It was suspiciously quiet for eight o'clock on a

Moncton Station in 1897. The twentieth century took its toll but rail carriages still roll in and out of these once-mighty railway lands. Photo: Unknown

Saturday evening, but perhaps threatening skies were keeping people indoors.

I bumped into a young man on the sidewalk, leaving his job at the liquor store, and after seeking his advice on where to eat we got into conversation. It turned out he'd spent the previous summer working as a security guard at the Algonquin Hotel, the next stop on my journey. He gave such a glowing account of the place and raved about playing golf on its famous course for free that I almost began to wish I was heading there to work, and not just spend a night under its hallowed roof. As we parted, I promised to try his restaurant recommendations, but not before I'd explored the length of Main Street, which parallels the riverbank and forms a tidy border to the southern edge of downtown.

Moncton is refreshing in the low-key way it fosters bilingualism. I heard French and English everywhere I went, and locals flipped back and forth between the two with ease. Although my French is on the poor side of lousy, I spoke a few words and did a little shopping without hassle or being made to feel stupid. I soon learned, however, that many people had endured more than enough of the Francophone Summit. This was not because of any language issue, but because of the paranoid, American-style security that came with it. One man told me he was standing on the roof of his downtown business premises, enjoying a cigarette as he did three or four times a day, when his cell phone rang and a sharp voice told him to "get the hell off that roof right now!"

As darkness fell, I arrived at the Pumphouse, the recommended brew pub on Orange Street, carrying a small thirst and a huge appetite. I ordered the acclaimed smoked turkey wood-oven pizza and a pint of cream ale, and was promptly satisfied by both.

Perhaps the evening was set up by the New Brunswick tourism authorities, but the people in that pub could have given any Friendly Manitobans a cheerful run for their money. I was soon hauled into the conversation at a nearby table and found myself sitting next to a very large man named Wade. He was bursting with nervous energy, his left foot bouncing rapidly on the floor, and he quivered all over, like an idling bus waiting for someone to climb aboard.

As a seasoned employee of the Department of Fisheries and Oceans, Wade put me right on a few maritime things. First, I needn't bother going down the street to see the tidal bore because since they built a causeway the river had silted up and the bore is now just a ripple of its former self. No, he said emphatically, I'd be much better off staying put and helping them sing a few songs. So I did. We filled the room with nautical ballads and I surprised the assembly with my rendition of "Barrett's Privateers," which I meant to sing in Halifax, but never mind. I met some wonderful characters, such as Shirley, who came in and, in a surprisingly chipper voice, told the group she'd been robbed again, for the third time that month. Sean, the pub's owner, had sage advice: "Shirl, ya gotta go home and ya gotta stay there!"

Good company was certainly a thief of time, and I left the place in the small hours of a warm, humid morning. Turning the corner onto Main Street, I was amazed to see that I was far from being the last one to call it a night. The road was a colourful, noisy torrent of cruising automobiles, their windows all down to let scores of parading pedestrians feel the throbbing music that poured forth. I sat on a bench outside a busy fast food restaurant to witness this nocturnal spectacle: Saturday night live, in downtown Moncton. Better by far, I suspected, than the small tidal bore I'd missed on the river.

After watching for a few minutes, I became aware of someone sitting next to me, quite close. It was Kevin, a man I'd met briefly in the pub, and he said downtown was like this every weekend. He also told me he was gay and wondered aloud if I was, too. I had to disappoint him in that department, and listened sympathetically as he mourned the wee size of Moncton's gay community. Then I stood up, wished him well, shook hands firmly and went back to the Beauséjour to sleep.

I couldn't reach St. Andrews by rail, as the passenger service had stopped running in December, 1994. The bus made only one daily return trip and wouldn't get me back in time for my next train, so I called a rental car office and was soon behind the wheel of a shiny blue, mid-sized GM product.

I drove along Highway 2, a toll road, with the windows rolled down, enjoying the rural splendour of New Brunswick countryside. Green pastures gleamed in the bright sunlight, late summer wildflowers swayed along the roadside, and birds flew back and forth high above rolling woodland. Had I turned down the FM rock station, I'm sure I would have heard Sunday morning church bells ring from each village I drove past.

I couldn't help thinking what a nice train ride this would have been, as surely it once was. The Saint Andrews & Quebec Rail Road was formed in 1836; soon after there was pressure to push the New England railroad network through Maine, New Brunswick and Nova Scotia to an ice-free harbour to berth European shipping. These lines wove a crucial network for distributing Nova Scotia coal.

In June, 1889, a train arrived in Saint John from Montreal, marking the completion of the Canadian Pacific Railway as a coast-to-coast railway. By that time, Saint John had become a key player in the railway industry and local companies, such as Harris and Allan, were kept busy, employing around three hundred men to build top-notch rolling stock. The Prince of Wales (the future King Edward VII) used one of the firm's first carriages on his state visit to Canada in 1860.

During the early 1940s this was one of the busiest stretches of single-track rail on the continent, bringing thousands of troops here to catch a boat ride to the war.

New Brunswick enjoys a lengthy railway history. Even the provincial Fires Act uses it as an anchor when it states "...a camp fire permit is not required by a person, who, for the purpose of obtaining warmth or cooking food, ignites a camp fire in or within one hundred metres of the centre of track of a railway." Tempted as I was to pull over to the side of the road and roast a marshmallow or two, I drove on.

I arrived at St. Andrews in the full heat of midafternoon, after covering 161 miles and getting lost around St. George. The fault, I thought, was all mine, but the third person I asked for directions confirmed that the map I had was a poor one.

Cruising into St. Andrews that warm Sunday afternoon was like entering another era. With well-kept gardens and brilliant white paintwork on its clapboard houses, picket fences and five churches, this little seaside town founded by loyalists in 1783 is vintage postcard material. A few settlers dismantled their homes in Castine, Maine, floated them across the bay on barges, and rebuilt them on lots where they stand to this day. The town has earned its designation as a National Historic District and clearly aims to keep it.

Finding the Algonquin Hotel proved easy enough, perched as it is at the top of the hill overlooking the tidy network of streets and lanes leading down to the harbour and waterfront of Passamaquoddy Bay. And what a quaint pile it is, with steep-pitched red roofs and smart black-and-white Tudor-style walls, surrounded by a verdant spread of lawns and bright flower beds of red, yellow and blue. A fresh ocean breeze ruffled the leaves of the birch trees, but it was far from chilly.

Built in 1889 by the St. Andrews Land Company as an Atlantic resort for New England's and Canada's elite, and taken over by the CPR in 1900, the Algonquin has weathered the ebbs and flows of mixed fortune. One Saturday lunch time, on April 11, 1914, a spark from a roofer's brazier set fire to the place and destroyed much of it. The hotel reopened on June 15, 1915, with extensive additions and a plush new verandah (called the Passamaquoddy verandah, after the bay), now the hotel's main dining area.

For more than a century the hotel stayed open only from May to October, but since 1996 it has offered winter breaks and business retreats, largely for New Brunswickers and Elderhostel groups.

The Algonquin Hotel, as genteel as a maiden aunt sitting pretty in crime-free St. Andrews. Photo: Dave Preston

My room wasn't quite ready for me, so I took to the footpaths to explore the grounds. People sat on the shady verandah and the front lawn, and a few children splashed merrily in the outdoor pool, which the lifeguard told me was due to close for the season the following day. The tennis courts looked forlorn, but a couple of seniors amused themselves at the outdoor shuffleboard, and a three-hole putting green entertained a couple more guests.

A building dating from 1903, just across the front lawn, originally served as a games pavilion, but today there is a wooden "Casino" sign by its front door. Peering through a large window I saw chairs and tables set up for a meeting or conference, with not a gambling device i sight. I later learned from an employee that earlier this century *casino* was a term used for a place where visitors could play cards and board games, but with nothing more at stake than fun and, perhaps, pride.

Wandering around the back of the hotel I noticed another sign beckoning me into a small gym, cool and dark with pink venetian blinds at the windows and a hot tub next door. Across the hall, the Lads and Lassies Family Hair Salon and Tanning Bed was just as quiet. A couple of sleek vinyl chairs were ready, but no one was getting trimmed or tanned while I was there.

A large, handsome building, put up in 1917 just behind the hotel, provides accommodation for some of the 250 staff, including several teenagers who sat beside it on the grass that afternoon, giggling over their magazines and cans of pop.

I crossed Carleton Street, leaving the hotel property, to a white cottage called Pansy Patch that featured a peculiar turret on its low roof. It's a bed and breakfast home that includes a restaurant and art gallery, so I opened the little gate, stepped up to the hefty front door and knocked. Theresa, an employee, showed me around and pointed out a long oak mantle carved with a verse from the sixteenth-century English poet Edmund Spenser:

Now faire betyde who here abyde and merrie may
    they be
And faire befalle who in this halle repaire in courtesie.
From morne till nighte be it darke or bright we banish
    droll and dree.
Come sit beside our hearth tis wide for gentle
    companie.

The woman responsible for the building and meticulous decoration of Pansy Patch in 1911 was Kate Reed, an Ontario-born aesthete and artist. She was commissioned to refurbish the grand CPR Hotels and scoured Europe for the desired antiques, paintings and furniture. (She also decorated the royal train coach that carried the Duke and Duchess of Cornwall across Canada in 1901.)

More rooms awaited guests in the cottage next door, built in 1856. The whole place is delightfully twee — ideal, I think, for someone like my mother, who would sip her tea until the faeries came home.

Almost two thousand people call St. Andrews home. You can still buy a building lot here for less than most of us would pay for a new car. A local RCMP officer claims it also has the lowest crime rate in Canada, which merely adds to the appeal.

Genteel and subdued as it may appear on its tweedy surface, the town stands ready and able for tourism with more than five hundred rooms available for visitors, half of them in The Algonquin. I eventually checked into a comfortable ground-floor suite opposite the ice and laundry room, which reminded me I had some laundry to do. I put my underwear on top of the ice machine to dry — partly because I hadn't the required coins for the dryer and partly because I wanted to test the low crime-rate claim, but mostly because I'm cheap.

Roaming the hotel, eerily peaceful though numerous guests milled about the place, I came upon the library, a dignified spot that's brassy and lacy, where guests are encouraged to enjoy a lunch or beverage surrounded by books and bathed in a golden beam or two of late afternoon sunshine. The hotel is certainly a restful place, sitting on the vacation spectrum at the opposite end to Club Med. I continued, through a long and airy hallway, past glass cases of artifacts and press clippings that detailed the hotel's history, and down a few steps to the "arcade level" to find The Right Whale Brew Pub and Restaurant. It was empty, but looked like it might be cheerful if the timing was right.

The Algonquin alone was worth the drive to St. Andrews, but after a light meal of tea, fresh fruit and lemongrass soda water, I set off for the other good reason I'd come here: the vacation home of William Cornelius Van Horne.

A large, robust man of Dutch-German descent with ice-blue eyes, Van Horne worked as general manager of the Chicago, Milwaukee & St. Paul Railroad when George

William Van Horne—artist, visionary, and ruthless rail boss. Photo: Glenbow Archives NA-2077-1

Stephen, first president of the CPR, went looking for someone special to push a railway over the Canadian Shield, to the north and west of Lake Superior. Van Horne came highly recommended and due to his "great mental and physical power" commanded a salary of fifteen thousand dollars a year, astronomical for that period. Not yet forty years old, Van Horne began work on the first day of 1882, promising to build five hundred miles of track across the prairies before the end of summer. He shunned adjectives and spoke in short, punchy sentences, leaving behind such aphorisms as "The biggest things are always the easiest to do because there is no competition."

A ruthless railway general, Van Horne controlled an army of five thousand men and seventeen hundred teams of horses, organizing the required supplies and accommodations. He described the desert to the east of Fort William as "two hundred miles of engineering impossibilities," but his crews laid track at the rate of three miles a day, forcing rails more than four hundred miles across Saskatchewan and adding at least a hundred miles of branch lines into the bargain. The railway penetrated the Rocky Mountains by the end of that first year.

He spent his winters in a sumptuous mansion bought in 1890 on the northwest corner of Stanley and Sherbrooke in Montreal's exclusive "Golden Square Mile." Summers, however, found him with his wife, daughter and son at an idyllic estate he purchased around the same time, on five-hundred-acre Ministers Island just off the northeast shore of the peninsula that forms St. Andrews. Van Horne would arrive by train, naturally, in his private car on the old Saint Andrews & Quebec Rail Road from McAdam to St. Andrews. Then, at low tide, he would take a horse and carriage to the island.

For some reason, I spent about five minutes singing what little I know of "Over the Sea to Skye", on the drive from the hotel, across Mowat Drive and down Bar Road. On the eighth chorus I rattled onto a rough gravel parking lot by a rocky beach. There I met Marie Hansen, who works for the Ministers Island Advisory Committee that administers the estate for the province. Since 1993 it has offered guided public tours from June to October. About a dozen people in half as many vehicles were there to take the evening tour, and a couple of hikers showed up at the last minute, as Marie and her colleague collected the admission fee. No one is allowed to cross on foot so I offered the young women, holidaying from Scotland, a ride in my car.

No bridge or fabricated causeway extends to the island, and boaters have no formal access. The tall wooden poles of old herring traps rise out of the water at several points around the bay, but from a distance the island seems to be untouched, with hardly a trace of civilization except for the lane that leads up from the beach and disappears into a dense thicket.

Motorists are led the five or six hundred yards across the ocean floor in convoy at low tide, with a guide in the lead vehicle and another bringing up the rear. The seabed lies under twenty feet of water at extreme high tide, so the two-hour tours must be chaperoned and carefully timed.

Van Horne avidly smoked Cuban cigars and eventually had one named after him with his picture on the band, but no smoking is allowed anywhere on the whole island now, as it could take hours to get a fire truck here, depending on the tides.

The "summer cottage," as he described it, named Covenhoven after his father, is a substantial home of some fifty rooms. It was built in three stages, beginning around 1890, from sandstone hewn just yards away on the shoreline.

At one time, there were twenty-two buildings on the property, including a farm, but now just half that many remain. About ten miles of carriage trails cover the island, but there's barely a trace of the sweeping driveway that once brought Van Horne and his guests to the front of the house, around perfect lawns he forbade anyone to walk over. Gone, too, are the greenhouses where Van Horne grew enormous peaches, testing the flavour himself each day before offering them to visitors. The current garden is little more than roughly cut grass, with a few surviving bushes and flowering shrubs. Unchanged, however, is the magnificent view of the ocean stretching southwards to Maine.

Before electricity came to the island in the 1950s, the homestead made its own power in a small shed in the backyard. A device dripped water onto carbide pellets to produce combustible gas that was stored and pressurized, then fed by pipe to the house. The water was drawn from a deep well by a tall, Dutch-style windmill that relinquished the job to a kerosene engine on windless days. An underground storage tank then piped it to various points around the estate, including a couple of fire hydrants.

A caretaker lived on the premises until the 1970s. Now it's home to no one. Thanks to a new roof, which cost $140,000 a few years ago, the place is dry, but longs for extensive restoration. The leaded windows of three-inch panes bow and bend with age, paint curls away from walls and ceilings, and patches of fallen plaster reveal the lathwork behind. In some rooms the original paint holds fast, including a decorative frieze that Van Horne, an accomplished painter, completed for his son's third birthday on July 29, 1910. It shows a Dutch scene with children being chased by a dog and a farmer; boys are running one way and girls the other.

All the paintings in the home are by Van Horne, with the

Detail of a frieze that William Van Horne painted on a bedroom wall for his son's third birthday. Photo: Dave Preston

exception of two: a rendition of the driving of the last spike at Craigellachie and a 1908 painting by Van Horne's friend, George Mathews, showing the house and flower gardens. On at least one occasion, Van Horne completed an entire painting in one night, in order to tease his guests when they saw it the following morning. He apparently needed very little sleep, and from the seventeen bedrooms in the home he chose the one downstairs off the main entrance hall, even though there was no downstairs bathroom. His wife slept upstairs at the other end of the house, in a room with fitted closets and glassed-in compartments that kept her hats free of dust.

Adeline, Van Horne's daughter, lived in the home until her death in 1941. The estate was later sold to a syndicate of ambitious Ohio businessmen. They aimed to set up a grand hunting lodge, but they soon discovered that there was very little game to aim at on the island. (Today, a herd of about seventy white-tailed deer roam the grounds.) Unfortunately, the syndicate made several garish renovations to the house before they left. Much of the original woodwork, lightly stained or oiled, received heavy coats of paint, some of which can only be described as bloody awful. To add insult to injury, an ugly bar was also installed, and although two of the bathrooms retain their original brass and porcelain fittings, the third appears cheaply modernized.

An American developer bought the estate in 1972 and it sat idle until an auction five years later, at which the province stepped in to save the day and around six hundred artifacts, but not before more than three hundred items had been sold to private collectors.

Our tour group walked across the garden to a hefty, two-storey circular bathhouse, draped in the remains of wild roses. A huge fire pit occupies the middle of the upper level, with chains overhead for suspending a copper flue. Downstairs, several wooden changing cubicles offer a little privacy from the windows around the building. Beach stone, quarried just below, was used to build the bathhouse, and the resulting rectangular hole, about twenty feet wide by thirty feet long, forms a saltwater swimming pool that fills twice a day. Lilacs and lupins border a pathway down to the pitted, red sandstone beach. This small quarry also supplied Van Horne's headstone, which he chose himself before his death in 1915. He is buried at his birthplace, Joliet, Illinois.

Before leaving the island we were shown the remains of the farm that kept the house supplied with produce and dairy goods. The huge wooden barn is about sixty feet high and covers more than nine thousand square feet of land. It was one of the largest in the country when built in 1898 at a cost of around $20,000. Unemployed shipbuilders were used for the construction and their craftsmanship, enforced and approved by their exacting boss, has stood the test of time beautifully.

Sunset warmed the hills to the northwest as we returned to the mainland, with less than an hour to spare before the tide swept back over the rocks and seaweed. I dropped off my hitchhiking passengers, whom I now knew as Fiona and Katrina, at their bed and breakfast place, and I returned to the Algonquin. Peeking into the laundry room, I gave the low crime-rate claim my seal of approval as I pulled my underwear from the top of the ice machine, warm and dry.

The next morning, at nine-thirty, I met the hotel's general manager, Andrew Turnbull. Employed by CP since 1982, he lives in a house on the hotel property and has seen a few changes since coming here in 1993. The addition of conference facilities aims to extend the season and increase room occupancy during the cooler months, he told me. The average stay for guests at the hotel is three days, and Turnbull admitted the Algonquin is favoured by an older, conservative crowd. The resort is recovering from a lean period during the early 1990s, and he believes a rosy future is teed up on the golf course.

The course has certainly gone a few rounds with the golfing elite — the game's been played here since 1893. Three clubhouses occupy the course and the original, one-room cabin is claimed to be the oldest single-purpose clubhouse in Canada. The latest building is a plush restaurant and pro shop. The course offered eighteen holes, plus nine, but fifty acres of land were added and the celebrated Thomas McBroom recently designed a new, 6,900-yard, par seventy-two course. CP, as the largest owner-operator of golf courses in Canada, should know what they're doing.

A visit to this renowned turf was in order, so I jumped in the car and set off, according to the directions: "Turn right, head out and you can't miss it." Minutes later, well out of the parking lot, I realized that right and left are subjective terms. My right turned out to be wrong, and I was soon in the middle of the town, pulling up in front of a white cottage to ask an old lady sitting in a chair on her front stoop, brilliant as the morning sunshine in her orange cardigan, for directions. Talk is cheap but she didn't hear enough of it and had plenty to give in return. After chatting about how many times she played the course and how nice it all is but it's not the same and how she hopes to goodness they won't ruin it with all this new redesign and landscaping, I finally found out how to get there, and bid her farewell.

Asking for permission to roam at will across the manicured greenery, I was offered the use of a golf cart and a driver to go with it. Curtis was eighteen years old, and his duties included fetching golf carts for guests and caddying a bit. But he's not a golfer. Deep down he's a snowboarder with plans to move to Whistler Mountain in B.C. and live a life packed with a bit more excitement than he currently finds in St. Andrews. But first, he took me around the course and showed me the ancient clubhouse, which turned out to be a bit disappointing: a small, locked-up building, with a new-looking layer of cedar siding and fresh stain. Only the red-brick chimney stack on the roof appeared to be of any real age.

Curtis drove me around a few of the more picturesque and challenging holes, such as number twelve, a steep, terraced fairway, only a hundred and fifty yards long, but with a green right at the edge of the ocean. I'm not a golfer, and I could imagine losing a lot of balls around here and a fair bit of temper.

I left the Algonquin around noon to make my way back to Moncton, driving Highway 3 north through more wonderful farmland and rural scenery, and passing close by the village of McAdam, which surely deserves tribute. Named after Irish-born lumberman turned politician John McAdam, the village was a key railway centre for the first few decades of the twentieth century. The CPR built one of their impressive "chateau-style" stations here at the dawn of the twentieth century, using local granite. After additions made during 1910 and 1911, the building became one of the busiest in the province, boasting a seventeen-room hotel upstairs. A dining room on the ground floor required almost thirty young ladies from the area to serve the finest food and drink to guests. The station had the usual men's and women's waiting rooms, a busy lunch counter and — being close to the Maine border — a customs and immigration office. The station also had a police department and a small jail for those who earned it.

At one point, sixteen passenger trains came through McAdam every day, taking people to and from St. Stephen, St. Andrews, Saint John, Woodstock, Edmundston and Brownville Junction Maine, with long-distance runs to Montreal and Boston. The CPR employed 650 McAdam residents in its heyday, but that went the way of all good things. The last passenger train left the station in 1981, as a lone bugler stood on the platform and played taps. By then, barely a handful of locals could name the railway as their employer. The station became a historic site and was featured on a stamp in 1988 as part of a series commemorating architectural heritage.

Highway 3 took me up to the Trans-Canada and my appetite chose the Fredericton exit soon afterwards, where I had a late, leisurely downtown lunch in a sidewalk café on Queen Street.

Swooping down off Highway 1 some hours later into the outskirts of Moncton, I ran into heavy traffic and started to get a little bit concerned as I had less than an hour to return the car and get to the station for the 6:10 p.m. train. Fortunately, the rush hour was more of a rush minute and traffic speed soon picked up again, giving me ample time to find the car rental office and let a nice employee drive me down to the station.

Moncton
~to~
Quebec City

MONCTON STATION BUBBLED WITH ACTIVITY AT SUPPER TIME, POSSIBLY for the first time in twenty-four hours. A crowd almost covered the platform. Some sat on the hot, black asphalt, but most of the older passengers sought out the shade along the station wall.

Although Quebec City wasn't on a direct route from the Maritimes to the West Coast, it had one of the country's finest hotels and I was determined to see it. The staff at VIA Rail gave me two options: I could take the train from Moncton to Montreal, then board another train to Quebec City, a total distance of 1,005 miles, or I could shave about 370 miles and several hours off the journey by getting off the train at Charny, just across the river from Quebec City, and taking a bus the rest of the way. The latter option sounded quite attractive, but lost its charm — became downright ugly in fact — when I realized the stop at Charny was scheduled for 5:07 a.m. I decided to take the train the whole way. After all, I'd come to ride the rails and if anyone needed beauty sleep, it was me.

On October 24, 1903, the National Transcontinental Railway Act was passed, opening the way for the Grand Trunk Railway to build a line from Moncton, New Brunswick, to Quebec. Some ninety-odd years later, the line between Moncton and Montreal is still in good use. For my trip I climbed aboard the No. 15, a continuation of the train that brought me to Moncton from Halifax. This time it had fourteen cars pulled by locomotives No. 6414 and No. 6456, a detail that matters to people who enjoy reading about trains, I had discovered, so I started collecting such information.

Travellers spending the night on board a VIA train have several options open to them, depending on their budget and nocturnal demands. The cheapest way is to sit in the day coach and pull a blanket over yourself. The dayniter car, somewhat like an airline cabin, offers a bit more room with stretch-out seats and leg rests, pull-down trays and overhead lights. Next step up the ladder to comfort and privacy is the sleeper car (there are two types of VIA Rail sleeper car: the Manor and the Chateau — both are very similar in comfort and design but have different room configurations). The sleeper car's basic accommodation is the section: two wide seats face each other by day and by night become bunk-style beds, curtained from the aisle by heavy grey drapes fastened with Velcro and buttons. Passengers lie parallel to the track, along the direction of travel, usually with their heads towards the front of the train. The upper berth is reached by a short removable ladder and an attendant sees to all preparations, making the bed up on request, often while passengers are in the dining car or watching a sunset from the dome of a park car. The roomette, with its sliding solid door, is a small cabin for one person. A folding seat flips down into a bed at night and tucked tightly beside it is a small sink and vanity unit.

For this leg of the journey, a scheduled run of just over fourteen hours to Montreal, I indulged in a fifth option: a double room. I was assigned to Room D in Car 20, the Chateau Richelieu. Like most of the other sleepers that VIA uses, it was built in the mid-1950s, but after a renovation and restoration or two, it still possessed the means to pamper a modern traveller. I found two very comfortable folding armchairs and a small, stainless steel sink with three mirrors above it and three faucets: hot, cold and drinking water. A separate toilet cubicle was tucked behind a slim door, with overhead storage space on top and two hidden bunk beds. A closet about two hands wide stood just through the door and a few coat hooks dotted the walls. The lights, fan, heat and air conditioning were controlled by a vertical bank of switches and knobs. With a Kleenex dispenser, a couple of large plastic drinking cups and complimentary bag of soap, shampoo and hair conditioner, my ablutions were all set for the next fourteen hours.

We pulled away from the station at around 6:30 p.m., only twenty minutes past schedule, and we were soon moving along at a fair clip. I explored the train, wobbling through many sleeper cars with narrow corridors, my shoulders bouncing off the walls at regular intervals. A few lost souls appeared before me, still in search of their seats or their rooms, or their mates. Numbers on the end door of each car, such as *0020* helped us keep track, though it was all too easy to forget which way led to the dining car.

Our train had a staff of fifteen, plus the two engineers. Two service attendants handled three sleeper cars between them, and two more staff handled the three coaches. One person was assigned full time to the park car at the back, tending to its bar and lounge.

I eventually reached the park car and admired the artwork. When CP ordered the equipment for *The Canadian*, in 1953, they had the foresight to commission eighteen of Canada's best-known contemporary artists to paint murals for each of the eighteen park cars. Each artist was assigned a national or provincial park — hence the name — from which to draw inspiration, and each was given $1400 and a year to complete the job.

The murals, painted on canvas, then glued to metal panels and riveted to the car's frame, included a map showing the park's location in Canada. L.R. Batchelor from Montreal did all the lettering, though the artists signed their work.

Damage was inevitable. The walls of the cars are subject to constant vibration, condensation, spilled drinks and food, and the rubbing of passengers' heads and other body parts. In 1984 the paintings were restored.

I was alone in the park car and stood for a minute staring through the window of the rear door, watching track disappear into the distance as if it were two lines of thread being pulled from an endless spool beneath my feet.

After helping myself to tea, I sat and scanned the newspapers and magazines. No newsies peddle their wares these days, but a vending machine at the end of the dome car dispenses batteries, decks of cards, aspirin, toothbrushes and toothpaste.

On the wall of the park car, a vertical bank of clocks housed in stainless steel showed the six time zones from Newfoundland to British Columbia. We would cross from Atlantic to Eastern Time as we reach Matapedia, just inside the Quebec border.

Leading off the park car, beneath the observation deck upstairs, a small, glassed-in area had room for a dozen passengers to sit. It had a bar and a TV, hinged to the wall to save space. The place was empty and quiet until a greeting from John, the service attendant in charge, broke the silence. We chatted for a minute about his bar menu and the fact that he'd memorized each of the three videos that are shown on the TV. I left him to polish his stainless steel countertop and climbed the short, narrow staircase to the observation deck, where I found a few passengers watching New Brunswick roll by at sixty miles an hour. The promise of a colourful sky grew stronger as the sun dipped behind the trees we were passing, some quite close to the track. Now and again we'd see a clearing, or a small stream, and soon the lights of farmhouses and distant homes sparkled a little brighter across the fields.

John made a brief appearance to say it was dinnertime, and I certainly didn't need inviting twice. I made my way to the nearest dining car, and stood in line behind a small group of people already selecting supper from a short buffet menu of soup, bread and a pasta dish. The sunset, flaring madly behind the northwest horizon ahead of the train, gave me a dinnertime show that made me forget I was sitting alone. The food was good and abundant. I'd come at first call partly to stop the growling in my stomach and also to beat the hungry hordes that would surely fill the room for the evening. But they never came. Breakfast, said the attendant as I left, could begin as early as 6:00 a.m. when the park car would have a complimentary buffet.

As darkness fell, I returned to the dome car, passing the sections already set up for sleeping, with people coming and going in various stages of night attire. Train travel, at least on this train, encourages a fair degree of informality. Folks in the coach were bedding down fully clothed, with blankets and pillows, and most seemed quite comfortable as they read or chatted to each other.

I wandered back down to the park car and stuck my head into the bar, where two couples sat with cans of beer, watching an Irish movie on television. Passengers can smoke in the bar, the only place it's allowed on the train. Not wishing to partake in canned beer, smoke or *The Waking of Ned Devine* (which I'd seen), I climbed back up to the observation deck, almost dark now save for the glow of a few safety lights.

I sat alone at the front and watched intently as the train headlights burrowed into the soft gloom ahead. Trackside weeds and branches appeared suddenly and were gone just as quickly. It would be impossible to stop in time for a deer or a stray cow. Or a bandit. This neck of the woods had seen crime. One black November night in 1967, two armed men took eighty thousand dollars from a safe in the baggage car of *The Scotian*, a Canadian National train bound for Halifax from Montreal. As the seventeen-car train was passing through Boleil, shortly after midnight, the men entered the baggage section, tied up the baggageman, grabbed the loot and jumped off at St. Lambert, just across the St. Lawrence River from Montreal.

As if marking an anniversary of this notorious hold-up, the train shuddered to an abrupt halt. Pressing my face against the cold glass to peer into the night, I saw the name *Charlo* on a station sign. Someone got on or off, though the platform was too dark to see anything clearly. Two minutes later we pulled away, with baggage car presumably intact.

At Campbellton, our next halt at around 10:20 p.m.,

most of the staff not busy converting seats into beds got off the train for a smoke or a chat on the station platform. The locomotives took on fuel and the sleeper cars took on water at our last stop before the province of Quebec. Following the advice of Gary, an attendant, I put my watch back an hour to Eastern Time, as we would soon roll over the time zone boundary in a quiet, unremarkable darkness. A stop in Matapedia, Quebec, I was told, would let us pick up a few cars and passengers coming off the Gaspé Peninsula train.

I returned to my room to see the chairs had been replaced by a lower bunk with sheet and blanket turned down, inviting me to slip inside. Lights out, it was darker and somewhat quieter than I thought it was going to be, but still sleep eluded me. My body rocked from side to side as the train accelerated or slowed down. Somewhere outside we passed the communities of Causapscal, Amqui, Sayabec and Mont-Joli. Although I saw the occasional sodium streetlight flash by, these places would remain only names on a railway schedule to me. I finally fell asleep around five o'clock in the morning, just a few minutes before we pulled into Charny, and I dimly recall feeling good about not choosing the bus option.

The park car, as promised, opened again for breakfast at six with a table full of prepackaged cereals, sliced bagels, oatmeal squares, pastries, tea, coffee and a variety of plastic juice tubs. Having slept only an hour or so, I clung to the sheets and shut my eyes tight against the brightening dawn, but time and scheduled arrivals wait for no slouch. So, after a refreshing shower in the surprisingly vacant, roomy and comfortable public facility, I met the challenge of drying my size XL body on a size S towel. My breakfast in the park car consisted of orange juice, two cups of tea and a couple of oatmeal squares as I watched the greyness of Montreal rise slowly into view.

The very first rail passenger service in Canada ran through this area. The Champlain and St. Lawrence Railroad Company's locomotive, the *Dorchester*, measured barely

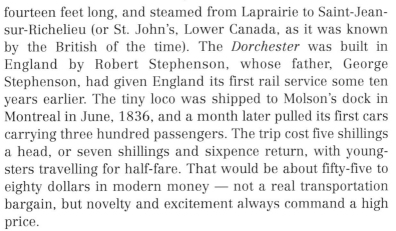

fourteen feet long, and steamed from Laprairie to Saint-Jean-sur-Richelieu (or St. John's, Lower Canada, as it was known by the British of the time). The *Dorchester* was built in England by Robert Stephenson, whose father, George Stephenson, had given England its first rail service some ten years earlier. The tiny loco was shipped to Molson's dock in Montreal in June, 1836, and a month later pulled its first cars carrying three hundred passengers. The trip cost five shillings a head, or seven shillings and sixpence return, with young-sters travelling for half-fare. That would be about fifty-five to eighty dollars in modern money — not a real transportation bargain, but novelty and excitement always command a high price.

Canada's first railway timetable, showing the *Dorchester's* schedule and fare, was published in Montreal's *Gazette* on August 6, 1836. The trip usually took about two hours, though on its initial run the locomotive ran out of water and burnt out a few boiler pipes, so the journey was considerably longer. The engine, assembled in Molson's Machine Shop, cost fifteen hundred pounds Sterling (about $200,000 today) and weighed five and a half tons. It ran on a track made of pine wood blocks with a metal strap nailed to the top edge, though this primitive line was replaced in the late 1870s by a T-rail made of iron, and eventually by the steel rails we ride on today.

The company added another engine soon afterwards, to meet the demand of day-trippers from Montreal. It was a U.S.-built affair called the Jason C. Pierce. Freight, of course, was a major concern to the railway owners; shipments of beef, pork, flour, meal and lumber were prominent. The popularity of the train ride came as a surprise to many, and within months the Canadian tourism industry was born, immediately howling for more routes, more vehicles and more sightseeing.

In the mid-1860s, the *Dorchester* was badly damaged in a wreck and remained in storage until 1873, when it was sold to a sawmill. All that survives of the original *Dorchester* is the brass nameplate, which turned up in a farmer's field near

Joliette in the 1880s. A couple of replicas of the diminutive locomotive were built in 1936 to mark the centenary of the *Dorchester's* first run. CNR apprentices made one of the replicas; the other, which sits in the Canadian Railway Museum in Saint-Constant, near Montreal, was put together by staff at the Château de Ramezay Museum in Montreal.

To reach the Island of Montreal a train must cross the mighty St. Lawrence River via the Victoria Bridge, formally opened on August 25, 1860, by the Prince of Wales, later to become King Edward VII. However, the first train had rolled across some months prior, on December 12, 1859, followed by the first passenger train five days later. The original structure consisted of a single-track iron tubular bridge, which posed severe ventilation problems. Entirely enclosed, it very quickly filled up with dense smoke and emptied of precious oxygen. Cutting a twenty-inch-wide slit let out some of the smoke, but the tube was replaced with a double-track steel bridge in 1898.

Quebec's freezing winters forged a certain innovation among the railway barons and saved a few thousand dollars worth of bridge construction. On January 31, 1880, the Quebec, Montreal, Ottawa and Occidental Railway (QMO & O) opened an ice railway between Longueuil, on the south shore of the St. Lawrence, and Montreal. Soon after the river froze solid, workers laid down temporary track on large timbers placed across the ice. During unfrozen months the QMO&O used a car ferry to cross the water. The ice railway operated every winter until 1883.

By the time I'd finished breakfast and walked back to my room the bed had disappeared again and the two chairs had returned. I sat and watched as we rumbled high over the river towards downtown Montreal, where we left the grey morning rain to pull into a long, black station. Everyone else was either more anxious to see Central Station than I was or, more likely, they were far better organized in stuffing their belongings into a bag or two and getting off the train. Perhaps they'd had more sleep, too. I was the last to disembark, but I had at least two hours before my connecting train to Quebec City, so even the world's best worrier, my mother, could rest assured that I'd catch it.

Downtown Montreal hasn't always been easy to reach by train. Squeezed into a curving corridor formed by the St. Lawrence River and the small "royal mountain" that gives the city its name, it proved a challenge to early railway builders. However, three more remote railway stations serviced it at the start of the century: the Bonaventure terminal of the Grand Trunk, the grand head office and Windsor Station of the CPR, and another CPR station called the Place Viger, a mile to the east near the waterfront.

Montreal Station—a huge frieze and words to the national anthem, but no left luggage lockers since a bomb went off in one. Photo: Dave Preston

A company called Mckenzie and Mann, which already owned and controlled more than twelve hundred miles of railway, decided the mountain could be tunnelled to bring trains right into the heart of the city.

Devised by Henry K. Wicksteed and engineered by the accomplished S.P. Brown, the first shafts for the tunnel were sunk in 1912. Unfortunately, there were not enough workers to continue the job as many men had been called up to serve in the First World War. Further delays came as the company struggled to pay damage claims filed by homeowners living above the tunnel. It took six years, but on October 18, 1918, the first train rolled through the mountain and drew into the Dorchester Street station.

CN opened Central Station, or Gare Centrale, a quarter-century later, on July 14, 1943. Since 1985, all passenger services to and from Montreal have run through this station, and my train slid into the musty, subterranean bowels of that building at eight-thirty on a wet Tuesday morning.

I hauled my bags out onto the grey, cheerless platform and struggled along to the nearest escalator. It wasn't the colourful welcome I'd imagined from a vibrant city renowned for its culture, but grandeur rose like a phoenix as the moving steps carried me out of the gloom and into Central Station's magnificent hallway, a cathedral of a place large enough to hold a hockey rink.

The place bustled with passengers, staff and city folks teeming out of the Metro station exit, or taking a shortcut through the station to neighbouring office towers and shopping centres. I felt the throbbing of trains coming and going beneath my feet and confirmed with a VIA employee that I had enough time to explore the station before descending again to climb aboard the No. 22 to Quebec City.

I checked my bags with a redcap at the luggage counter, the only alternative to carrying them around with me or having them stolen. Central Station has no lockers for passengers to store their luggage due to a tragic episode that took place on the morning of Monday, September 3, 1984. A bomb planted

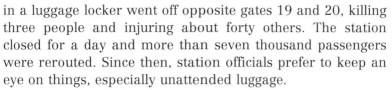

in a luggage locker went off opposite gates 19 and 20, killing three people and injuring about forty others. The station closed for a day and more than seven thousand passengers were rerouted. Since then, station officials prefer to keep an eye on things, especially unattended luggage.

I cut across the hall to the Panorama Lounge, where VIA's first-class passengers can bide their time between trains in relative comfort, with free drinks. A plaque on the wall is dedicated to Henry K. Wicksteed (1850–1927), crediting him with building the tunnel and the original terminal on this site.

Two huge friezes in bas-relief fill the walls at either end of the station. Their beige symbols and icons elegantly contrast with the attractive blue background, similar to Wedgewood pottery. The style is vaguely Egyptian, but the frieze details the lifestyle and industry of the country. The words to the national anthem, "O Canada," run around the bottom of the frieze in English at one end, and the French version appears at the other.

Just off the grand hall of the station I entered Les Halles de la Gare, a commercial concourse. The bright and lively deli counters and shops prompted me to take a photo, but I had barely removed my lens cap when a firm hand tapped me on the shoulder. I turned to see a uniformed security guard wearing a CN insignia and an expression he did not pick up in public relations training.

For a reason he did not make clear, photography was not allowed. The irony of the situation — this complex is eminently photogenic, having won the Concourse Commerce Jury's Grand Prize in 1998 for its design — eluded my new friend with the dark blue uniform and the matching scowl. My mumbled French seemed lost on him, too. Montreal is the second-largest French-speaking city in the world, after Paris, so I forgave his lack of English. With a few waves and gestures, I eventually got across the idea that I was writing a book about the railways and hotels, and a quick shot of the Halles would complete my research. He said — at least I'm fairly sure he said — that I had to go with him to the CN headquarters in a neighbouring building and make an appointment to see a certain Monsieur Richardson to obtain official permission. My jaw dropped. I sighed a universal sigh, looked at my watch and gave a slight shake of my head. *Et voila!* Realizing that to trail off to see Monsieur Richardson would be a waste of time for all three of us, he straightened his scowl and made an executive decision on the spot. I was granted exactly two minutes and one photograph, which I gratefully accepted. Of course, no sooner had I taken my picture than a Japanese tourist stood at my shoulder and focused his camera on the same composition. The security guard gave me the kind of look he might have when pulling his navy blue pants out of a washing machine, only to realize they should have been dry-cleaned.

Legend has it this station was the scene of a shootout, though I can't confirm this. Some children supposedly released a bunch of helium-filled balloons that floated up to the ceiling and gave cleaners one hell of job trying to remove them. Sharpshooters were brought in late one night to pop the balloons with air rifles. I'm willing to bet that Monsieur Richardson didn't know anything about it.

Having circumnavigated the great hall, I took the weight off my feet by sitting in one of two reclining seats, just like those on commuter trains that run along the Montreal–Toronto corridor. As I watched a large screen made up of several smaller TV screens, a VIA rail promotional video flared up noisily, using both official languages. No one else came anywhere near the area, and I soon realized the seats were far too close to the screen to be practical, and were obviously part of the installation. Feeling hugely conspicuous and as much a part of the show as the images flashing before me, I sat and watched for a while. In a matter of minutes I crossed the whole country on a virtual train ride. The lobster traps of the Maritimes gave way to the soaring skyscrapers of Montreal, then gleaming Toronto led to the hard Canadian Shield of Ontario and the expansive Prairies, run amok with cowboys, horses and corn. The Rockies rose and fell into the Pacific shoreline as the virtual ride pulled into a Vancouver bathed in a sunset as golden as a senior's travel brochure.

Time flew, as I was having fun, and office workers and passengers who had fun watching me appeared slightly disappointed when I rose and made my way back to the luggage counter to recoup my baggage. I tipped the redcap a dollar per bag, which I thought appropriate, and his smile confirmed this decision. Either that or he was having a good day anyway, with or without my cash.

I boarded train No. 22, an abbreviated affair of just three cars pulled by locomotive No. 6905. The first-class front car was followed by two economy cars. I settled into seat No. 31 in car No. 1. The attendant seemed particular about such details but no one sat by me so I spread my bags and books out over the seat. The attendant was also particular about telling me how to break the window with a little hammer, cover the broken edges with my seat cushion and climb out to safety, should the need arise. Just like the other passengers he coached, I nodded nonchalantly and said I fully understood, as though escaping from a train wreck was something I did every week. I also promised not to break anything unless it was absolutely necessary.

Ever the explorer, or fidget, and having the benefit of a reserved first-class seat, I wandered back down the aisle to the second-class coaches to see life at the other end. The economy cars look similar to first class, or VIA 1 as it's known in railway parlance, but they are down a notch in the luxury stakes. My car, for example, had drapes, not that I liked them. It also had a complimentary bar service that began as soon as we reached fifteen miles per hour, which naturally sent me scurrying back to my seat at a similar speed.

Armed with a glass of Chardonnay I toasted *La Belle Province*, though few people here still refer to Quebec in this way. My complimentary VIA 1 lunch, served from a cart, consisted of a small but succulent salad with sun-dried tomato and oregano dressing, a fresh roll from the bread basket, and whatever I wanted from the bar cart.

The scenery outside my draped window seemed to have been made soggy by a heartless grey drizzle. There wasn't much to look at: rough agricultural land, corrugated for the most part by a series of drainage ditches occurring every forty feet or so. A few brown fields of seemingly forgotten corn leaned wearily, braving the elements, and solid stacks of birch firewood stood ready to melt the onslaught of winter. I found the VIA 1 bar cart a far more amusing distraction, as did most other passengers.

It rained most of the way. We stopped briefly at Drummondville and Charny, and about three hours after leaving Montreal, we came to a halt in Sainte-Foy Station, where a dozen or so people got off and a few others boarded. According to my little map and train schedule we were almost there, and I grew impatient to be off.

Two train stations serve Quebec City, if you're not too worried where the city boundary lies. The Gare du Sainte-Foy on Chemin de la Gare (Station Road, for those who don't speak French) lies, predictably, in Sainte-Foy. The other, at Gare du Palais, stands with equal geographic logic on Rue de la Gare du Palais in Quebec City proper, across a bridge.

The Quebec Bridge spans the St. Lawrence River and received its first mention by name on May 23, 1853, but thanks to funding problems and a general lack of interest (not to mention politics), the National Transcontinental Railway didn't open it for use until sixty-five years later. Mishaps plagued the thing. Work began in 1905, but on August 29, 1907, seventy-five men lost their lives when the southern span collapsed. In 1911 the Dominion Government took over and the St. Lawrence Bridge Company continued working to a new plan. On September 10, 1916, the suspension span buckled and fell while being lifted, plunging into the river and taking another ten souls with it. Finally completed in 1918, it captured praise and admiration as the world's longest cantilever bridge of the time. Canada Post paid tribute to the bridge in 1995 by including its image in a postage stamp series.

Brass, brick and polished floors make the Gare du Palais a palatial spot to wait for trains. Photo: Dave Preston

A few minutes before four in the afternoon, as per schedule, we pulled into the Gare du Palais. The dark concrete platforms were similar to those we left in Montreal, but smaller. The original station, built in 1879 to serve as the QMO & Q's Quebec City terminus, was replaced in 1916 by this current building, which temporarily closed in 1976 to let the suburban depot in Sainte-Foy inconvenience passengers. Demand, and perhaps a bit of common sense, led to its reopening in 1985. The bar cart had disappeared and I was ready to get off.

Quebec City
∼ to ∼
Montreal

QUEBEC SERVES UP MANY CULTURAL DIFFERENCES FOR THE VISITOR to celebrate. One is that you can't make a right turn on a red light. Another, which intrigued me as I stood at the station exit, is that cabs do not respond to the usual pedestrian hand signals. Nor do they respond to shouting, frantic waving or the piercing two-fingers-in-the-mouth whistle I learned in high school. They respond to their radio dispatchers.

About twenty of us train passengers celebrated this latter cultural difference that grey Tuesday afternoon, as we tried to get a ride from the station to somewhere else in the city. An enterprising young woman and I finally hijacked a cab as it dropped someone off at the station and failed to make its get-away. I shared the ride for five minutes up steeply winding, narrow streets and through a stone archway to the Château Frontenac. I paid my share, bid my accomplice bon voyage, and pulled my luggage out of the cab and into the impressive front courtyard of the hotel.

Samuel de Champlain certainly knew a good site for a building when he saw one. Landing in 1608, he founded Quebec City and put up a modest fort on this spot in 1620. A few years later Champlain's settlement became Fort St. Louis, then Château St. Louis. It was destroyed during an attack by Sir William Phipps and the British, then rebuilt by the French governor Comte de Frontenac in 1692. Again the British roughed it up and the chateau finally burned to the ground in

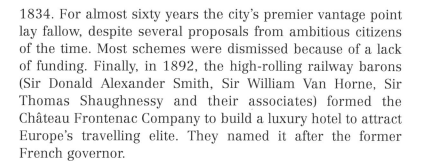

1834. For almost sixty years the city's premier vantage point lay fallow, despite several proposals from ambitious citizens of the time. Most schemes were dismissed because of a lack of funding. Finally, in 1892, the high-rolling railway barons (Sir Donald Alexander Smith, Sir William Van Horne, Sir Thomas Shaughnessy and their associates) formed the Château Frontenac Company to build a luxury hotel to attract Europe's travelling elite. They named it after the former French governor.

I'll get the word magnificent out of the way, as it's impossible to describe the Frontenac without using it at least once. One of CP's signature hotels, its design is based on the sixteenth-century royal chateaux found in the Loire Valley. Several of them, such as the Chambord, begun in 1520, had riotous rooflines with tall chimneys, pinnacles and dormers strewn about with finicky classical excess. The Italians are often blamed for this lavish influence. Other buildings, like the Château Fontainebleau, were a little more sober, and their steep roofs and robust chimney stacks were quite practical for the Canadian climate and for many CP hotel designs. Some claim the Frontenac was modelled after a lunatic asylum built in Buffalo, New York, by H.H. Richardson, but enough drawing-board gossip for now.

Suffice to say that architect Bruce Price, coaxed away from the United States in 1886 to design the Banff Springs Hotel for William Van Horne, still knew what he was doing six years later when he came to Quebec. After the hotel opened to much fanfare in 1893, it became the first stop in North America for many affluent visitors arriving here by ship from Europe. The CPR would then show this well-heeled crowd the delights of Canada, by train.

Since Price, other demi-gods of the architecture world, including Walter S. Painter and the Maxwell brothers Edward and William, have left their mark on the hotel during a series of expansions, renovations and decorations.

I entered the lobby and stood for a moment enjoying the rich ambience of oak panelling, gleaming brass fixtures, heavy wall sconces, curious oil paintings and enormous floral arrangements. The hotel reeked of class and appeared to be every luxuriant thing I was led to expect. Alfred Hitchcock arranged for a murderer to be killed here, in a celluloid manner of speaking. During the Second World War, Winston Churchill and Franklin D. Roosevelt planned the Normandy invasion under this very roof. Musician Pierre Marchand gave more than thirteen thousand concerts in this building. A man named Edmund Leonard set a residency record by living at the hotel for twenty-nine years and another man, Lionel Verret, set one by working here for more than fifty. The Château Frontenac had served many purposes, and all of them with class. It would certainly do for me.

I checked into Room 5147, a suite in the east end of the

The boardwalk by the Château Frontenac. By day, a delightful stroll, by night...beware of Elvis impersonators.
Photo: Dave Preston

The luxurious Frontenac—it's no wonder one guest lived here for almost thirty years. Photo: Dave Preston

building. It was at the end of a quiet hallway off the fifth floor, tucked under a section of the roof, as though it might have been servants' quarters at some time.

A short passage led from the front door to a living room with an armoire housing a TV, mini bar and drawers. A substantial desk with a phone and lights stood adjacent to it, and there were a couple of antique upholstered chairs. Two end tables with extravagant lights flanked a long, three-seater couch. A welcome note from the hotel manager, a box of fruit and a small box of chocolates sat waiting for me on the Duncan Phyffe-style coffee table.

An archway through a thick wall led to the bedroom with its king-size bed, side tables and lamps, another desk, an occasional table with another basket of goodies, and an armoire with another TV. Off the bedroom, a full bathroom with a tub and shower had been carefully built into the slope of the roof.

Deep, dark green carpet with a small star motif in a cream colour lavishly covered the floor and matched the fleur-de-lys wallpaper. There were beams overhead, painted cream to match the wallpaper. I've been in some attics, but this one took the biscuit. And the well-iced cake.

Two narrow windows looked westward from the suite onto a small, peaceful herb garden nestled on a flat roof perhaps ten feet below my room level, where parsley, sage, rosemary and certainly thyme grew between gravel pathways. Two other windows looked east, down the verdigris of the copper roof onto the bustling boardwalk far below, over Old Quebec and across to the town of Lévis, about a mile away on the far bank of the St. Lawrence.

I unpacked no more than necessary. It had been a long day, especially long considering the short night's sleep that came before it, so my attention fell onto the fruit and chocolate, which I nibbled as I tried out a thick, white bathrobe I pulled from the closet. Within minutes I lay in the steamy, wet cocoon of a candlelit bath, while a street performer's lilting melody wafted up from the boardwalk through the open window. I closed my eyes and said out loud: "I could get used to all this. Very easily."

(Of course, such indulgence has a down side. I fell asleep, only to wake up at 1:00 a.m. in a tub full of cold water with a hardened stream of candle wax stuck to my hairy leg. A state of affairs I'd never get used to.)

I slept the sleep of kings, in a suitably sized bed, and awoke to a bright and cheerful morning outside. My first area of exploration was the rooftop garden, and I was taken there by a private tour guide, a hotel employee named Nathalie. The only route was through a fourth-floor sash window, and a tight skirt and heels made the approach a slow and delicate one (for her, that is, not me). Executive chef Jean Soulard concocted the garden idea to provide a place where he could seek refuge occasionally and grow herbs and edible flowers for the hotel's Champlain Restaurant. He supervised its design and planting in 1993. A tiny electric fence around the garden discourages marauding pigeons. Of course, the small garden cannot possibly supply the quantity of herbs and edible flowers required to flavour or adorn the approximately three thousand meals the hotel prepares daily. But it improves the view from Room 5147.

Safely back inside the hotel, clutching an aromatic sprig of thyme, I ambled around the Frontenac, awed at almost every turn by the elaborate decor and attention to detail. Floors 12, 14 and 15, recently remodelled by international designer Alexandra Champalimaud, make up the *Entrée D'Or* — a collection of special suites and rooms for Entry Gold guests. Annie, the concierge, explained that "all the home touches are provided" for preferred guests, such as overnight shoe-shine and twenty-four-hour-a-day access to snacks and drinks in the common room. This privileged clientele also avoids the hubbub of the lobby downstairs. They come directly up to this "hotel within a hotel."

The sixth floor houses a spacious, tiled pool and spa, as well as a children's pool and large whirlpool tub, and its cool invitation struck me as something I should accept later that day. A permanent photo exhibit hangs on the second and third floors of the Citadel Wing, displaying the evolution of the Frontenac and some of the royalty and celebrities who have stayed here.

In 1993, a year-long celebration of the hotel's one hundredth anniversary brought guests and former employees from around the world, and the Frontenac appeared on a Canadian postage stamp issued in June that year, along with four other CP hotels (the Algonquin, the Royal York, Banff Springs and the Empress).

I descended more stairs to explore some of the function rooms. The ballroom, with its tidy proscenium stage and sparkling chandeliers, still serves as such about eight times times a year, but caters mainly to conferences and meetings.

It can seat up to eight hundred people.

The Salon Frontenac in the Riverview Wing is a fine example of one of the many banquet rooms, restored to its original mediaeval-style grandeur after the hotel's dramatic fire. On January 16, 1926, a blaze took hold of the building and fire-fighters watched almost helplessly. Bitterly cold weather froze water to the outside walls seconds after it left their hoses, turning the hotel into a gruesome ice palace for a while. Billed as a fireproof building (a major selling point for hotels at the turn of the century) the Frontenac suffered $760,000 worth of damage but remained structurally sound. The cause of the fire was never determined, though fireplaces throughout the hotel were deemed unsafe and it was forbidden to burn solid fuel. A few have since been converted to propane.

La Verchères, with its beautifully painted ceiling from 1924, once housed tropical plants and huge palms to set an exotic ambience for guests taking afternoon tea. Wedding parties tend to use the intimate and circular Salon Rose, with its glorious 180-degree views across the river.

Forty coats of arms from the city's founding fathers decorate Le Champlain dining room, which has its own kitchen.

During the Second World War, Churchill, Roosevelt and Mackenzie King met in the library, just off the dining room, which still appears the way it did in 1943. The hasty organization of that famous wartime summit meant approximately two thousand room reservations had to be cancelled within days, probably bringing a certain air of conflict much closer than it had been until that point.

In the main elevator lobby, a bank of three antique beauties work their way quietly up and down the tower. Close by, an old brass and glass mailing system made by the Cutler company of Montreal connects the floors, still pouring letters and postcards down into a collection box at its base.

At the west end of the main entrance lobby there is a small elevator vestibule, with old-fashioned lanterns to brighten its coffee-coloured walls. Above an antique, inlaid dresser, an oil painting shows an adversary of Frontenac's, Monseigneur de Laval. Dutch blue tiles lead up a few steps to the administration offices. The hotel has managed to marry differing styles — from the ancient and somewhat rustic, through the decorously opulent, to the sleek efficient.

Marble steps, twenty-two of them at the other end of the main lobby, took me down to the lower commercial concourse, where I found shops, galleries, hairdressing salons and agencies. The Café de la Terrasse offered Linguini aux Shiitakes on its doorway menu and, in French but literally translated here: "leg of lamb fed on salty pastures."

The menu served as a reminder that lunchtime was approaching, but I had things to see outside first, so I wrapped up my tour and headed for the front door. Heading south from the hotel I found a small park with an obelisk dedicated to General Wolfe, the English conqueror, and a broad, lengthy boardwalk known as Dufferin Terrace. I walked into the sunlight, peering occasionally over the green painted railings, down to the old port and docks far below.

I climbed 136 steps to a plaque marking *The Promenade des Gouverneurs*, a scenic walkway opened on September 9, 1960, by the country's tenth prime minister, John

Diefenbaker. I climbed a further forty-five steps, past wild hops growing just out of reach beyond a stainless steel fence, then up another forty-six, quite briskly as I wanted to get back for lunch. I climbed seven more and finally staggered into a circular lookout tower. Breathless, and not simply from the view, I mingled with dozens of tourists who seemed far less sweaty or exhausted than myself. They were from three tour buses that had conveniently driven to within a few yards of the lookout.

I lingered, taking in the broad landscape across to the famous Plains of Abraham. Despite the biblical sound, the Plains derive their name from Abraham Martin, a lad of Scottish descent who piloted boats along the St. Lawrence during Champlain's time and later settled down to run a few sheep and cattle on these pastoral tablelands. The locals called him Maître Abraham.

The British and French, notorious for not getting along no matter which side of the Atlantic they find themselves on, took to these fields in September, 1759, to beat the sense out of each other. Forty-eight hundred British troops under General James Wolfe quickly defeated about six thousand French troops and five hundred native Indians under Marquis de Montcalm. Both leaders were killed in the fray.

With the buses gone, the Plains grew eerily peaceful as I turned back to walk along to the Citadel walls. Built by a nervous British army between 1820 and 1831, the fortress affords a nice view down over the old city.

Almost two million people visit this historic site every year, but the day I visited the place belonged to me. (I'd begun to notice how many times I found myself alone on this trip, in places that were usually heaving with people. Odd.) I crossed the deep, dry moat on a steel catwalk and walked along the inner wall edge, being careful not to look down too often, nor up to the towering Frontenac that hallmarked the skyline.

Back down in the shady, cobbled streets of Old Town, I perused an alleyway full of artists and took a sidewalk table at a restaurant obviously popular with the locals. This is an old traveller's trick that had served me well in the past. However, I soon realized that here the waitresses served the locals first. The rest of us endured incredibly slow service, but having waited twenty minutes already and seeing that it was about my turn as everyone else was eating, I decided to stay. Just then, everyone around me lit up a cigarette or two, or ten. Quebec City, I read later, has the highest rate of lung cancer in Canada.

I began to suspect that I upset the waitress with my English accent when I ordered the French-Canadian pea soup and bread. She seemed to hold me personally responsible for Montcalm's defeat and brought me the food exactly fifty-five minutes later — forty minutes longer than it took them to fight the damn battle. Soup eaten, I left an appropriate tip and a few appropriate words with a couple of tourists I met on the way out.

The afternoon proved warm and weary as I explored the stoney length, breadth and width of Old Quebec, confirming that, indeed, the Château Frontenac looks imposing from all angles. Some hotels are immensely pleasing to look *from*, commanding spectacular views of the surrounding landscape. Some are spectacular to look *at*, and provide tourists with a photo opportunity almost as much as they provide local residents with an inspiring landmark and sense of community pride. The Château Frontenac is, quite truly, both of these.

I passed the Quebec Citadel Incline Plane, a short, steep railway opened in 1823 to haul people up and down the embankment from the port to the upper level where the Frontenac stands. A stationary steam engine supplied power until the late 1840s but these days a funicular railway using two cars takes people up from Lower Town to Upper Town, at a dollar or so per two-minute ride.

As twilight fell I found a small bar with thick stone walls and an enticing two-for-one deal on certain Québecois beers. I sipped a cool Fin du Monde, then another, wrote a few postcards, and in a burst of *joie de vivre* planned myself a *très jolie* night on the town.

The planning fell through somewhat, possibly because of the Fin du Monde. So I took a pizza back to my room where I pampered myself again with another long bath, serenaded by an enthusiastic Elvis impersonator on the boardwalk below. I finally made my way to bed and set a small alarm clock for 8:00 a.m. I had a train to catch in the morning.

The Gare du Palais is a cute little station, a petite chateau of a building — the kind you might see in a children's movie begging to be animated, with its twin towers and pseudo portcullis over the main entrance, a large clock in its forehead. Inside, the red bricks and blue-green paintwork create a bright and cheerful atmosphere. For my trip to Montreal I had a VIA 1 (first-class) ticket, so I stood in a short line with a few others while a mob of American tourists roamed the station at a loss, not sure where to go or whom they might ask, apart from each other, which they did repeatedly.

I enjoyed the moment. Years of civilized communication, summarized around the station in large words such as *Information*, *Tickets*, *Exit* and *Trains* went unheeded. There might not be a living telephone switchboard operator on this continent in a decade's time, but every last train station will *always* need a living person for passengers to ask.

Ushered by the attendant at train time, I made my way down to the platform and saw No. 23, another three-car affair: one first-class and two economy coaches. Settling into seat No. 31, the same I had coming to Quebec City, I began to unpack a few things for the ride when chaos poured in through the door. About thirty of the American tourists, now loosely organized into a herd with a common direction, rapidly filled the rest of the car, stuffing seats with bags, cameras and each other.

They sat anywhere and everywhere, oblivious to the fact that first-class seats are always pre-assigned. The VIA attendant, a small man with thick glasses, struggled his way

The Gare du Palais in Quebec City, built in 1916 and viewed here from the site of the original 1879 CP station.
Photo: Dave Preston

through and eventually identified the tour group leader. When he asked if her followers were all in the correct seats, she laughed and said, "Probably not."

"Lovely," he sighed, then spent the next ten minutes finding adjacent seats for three young Japanese women who waited by the doorway, smiling.

We were late setting off, something that Mark, the young attendant serving tea and coffee, couldn't explain, except to say that he was on his way home after a week's work and wanted the train to run on time as much as anyone. He joked with passengers, offered us cream and sugar with our drinking water, and he nicely animated the mandatory safety demonstration, showing us how to break a large train window with a tiny hammer and climb through using only a seat cushion for protection. He really made the exercise seem like a lot of fun — something I might like to try for myself one day soon.

We trundled past curious suburban landmarks such as the Colisée, former home of the NHL's Québec Nordiques, and the Hippodrome de Québec, where people still hope to win their fortune on horse races. The trundle grew into a smooth, steady roll, and we finally picked up enough speed to pass a cyclist on a nearby road who had been threatening to reach Montreal ahead of us.

The American tourists chatted merrily, obviously pleased with the train and its service. The group leader, a gregarious Goldilocks who had by now tried almost everyone's seat but her own, came and sat by me. Pleased with her flock, she told me things were going well for her on this leg of their Canadian adventure. VIA, in either of her pronunciations of the word, had earned a place on her Gold Star List, and perhaps even in her will. "We have Amtrak of course, but it's got such a bad name and you never feel very confident taking a group on it, but this service is first class." Mark beamed with job satisfaction and offered her more cream and sugar, without water.

When she left to go and compare maple syrups with one of her group, I reclined my seat and relaxed into the ride. The train had certainly been good enough for King George VI and Queen Elizabeth. On May 18, 1939, they began a royal tour of Canada, leaving Quebec City on a train using five cars from CP, five from CN and two vice-regal cars in royal blue. A pilot train carrying officials and the press went ahead, leaving Quebec City an hour before the royal train, and no other rail traffic was permitted during the interim period. CP and CN shared the prestige and the travel arrangements, using locomotives No. 2850 and No. 2851 for the royal and pilot trains respectively. No. 2850, with large, two-dimensional crowns affixed to the running boards, hauled the royal train right through to Vancouver, a total distance of 3,224 miles. The decorative crowns eventually adorned the entire 2820-2864 locomotive class, which, following royal approval, came to be

The Queen Elizabeth, the first hotel in the world to Give Peace a Chance, when John Lennon and Yoko Ono staged their famous bed-in. Photo: Dave Preston

known as Royal Hudsons. (One of these, No. 2860, has since served periodically on a coastal run in British Columbia, taking BC Rail passengers from Vancouver to Squamish.)

The scenery from my window looked unsurprisingly familiar to that which I'd seen on the way out, but under sunny skies it looked far more picturesque. The drainage ditches had dried, and plump cattle grazed contentedly on grass made emerald green by the rain of two days ago. The long piles of drying firewood, fuel for some far-off winter, appeared to be quite superfluous.

Montreal's Central Station platform looked grey, however, as we pulled in that afternoon. Exactly two minutes after hauling my bags off the train I had crossed the station, sidestepped the jostling crowds of Les Halles de la Gare and stood, regaining breath and composure, in the elevator lobby of the Queen Elizabeth. The room, with lush carpeting and immaculate mahogany panelling on the walls, seemed to be a thousand miles away from the harsh noise of the station just a few yards behind me. Within seconds I was heading for the main lobby two floors up.

I arrived ahead of check-in time, so I left my luggage with the bellman and toyed with the idea of taking my camera back out to the Halles, to spend an hour or two annoying security guards. I settled instead for a comfy chair in Les Voyageurs, a bar just off the hotel lobby. Taking a seat towards the back of this restful, deep pink room, I noticed the round wooden tables were topped with sections of nautical charts. Mine had the outline of James Bay, Victoria, a curving arm of land that protects the water of the famous Inner Harbour. I immediately thought of the Empress Hotel, my final destination, still some two and a half weeks and three thousand miles away. It was a sobering thought — my travel budget might not last, and without doing laundry my clothing certainly wouldn't. I changed my cocktail order for a soda water.

The Queen Elizabeth is famous for its martinis and cocktails, such as Manhattans and Rob Roys presented in extra-large snifters. It has served more than fourteen million of them over the last forty-odd years (the public relations person was paid to give me this information, so the least I can do is pass it on). The hotel bars have dished out about 760 tons of peanuts and pretzels during that period, and sliced or squeezed twenty-two million oranges, limes and lemons, give or take. Knowing full well it might compromise their statistics, I took my glass of soda without lemon, passed on the nuts and cracked open a book.

My room was on the eighth floor, compact and business-like yet comfortably fitted with modern furniture and with floral hints to the decor. The view to the rear of the hotel was also business-like — to the southeast, across a flat roof below and past rooftop parking beyond that. The huge, white Bell building stood to the left, the towering Place Bonaventure was dead ahead and the CN building grew into the sky to my right. I caught a glimpse of the St. Lawrence River between the two. The curtains, so often overlooked by a hotel's interior designers, functioned well. That is, they closed easily, met in the middle and made the room very dark. Many hotels have drapes that are nice to look at or match the bedspread but do not reduce the amount of light coming into a room. For those of us used to sleeping in rural areas, where the night sky is black and the nearest streetlight is five miles away, curtains matter. The room had a sexy black marble bathroom that soon had several unsexy items of my clothing in various stages of being laundered.

I heard a maid cleaning the room across the hall from mine, and following a polite request, she let me see the view from that room. It looked northwest, over René-Lévesque Boulevard, across a concourse and past the office tower that houses the VIA headquarters. A thin green slice of Mount Royal rose up into the low cloud beyond.

In 1874, when Montreal and its population of 120,000 constituted the largest urban centre in Canada, many influential eyes looked this way and the city became self-conscious of its image. Among other things, they asked Frederick Law Olmsted, the man who designed Central Park in New York City, to do something about the mountain.

Olmsted took this mile-long, half-mile-wide, 735-foot-high mass of glacial deposit (hardly a real mountain, but it's theirs to call what they wish) and divided the landscapes into eight areas that he named Underfell, Crags, Cragsfoot, Upperfell, Brackenfell, and so on, depending on their vegetation and natural features. In September, 1877, he presented a grand plan that took a dozen years to complete. In his words, the mountain presented the city with a "prophylactic and therapeutic agent of vital value." So there.

The city encroached over the years. Asphalt and concrete have climbed their defiant way up and around Mount Royal, but about five hundred acres of the summit has been left pretty much as an urban park should be. The area names that Olmsted used, so obviously English in origin, have long been forgotten and few but local historians recognize them. From the hotel window I could see the famous landmark steel cross and could hardly wait for nightfall when seventy-eight bright white lamps would light up each face. The maid, who barely spoke English, showed patience but could hardly wait for me to go back to my own room.

Unlike the Château Frontenac, a hotel that virtually demands to be both looked at and looked from, the Queen Elizabeth relies on a great location, at the heart of a tight downtown core with easy access to public transport. This is the largest hotel in the city with twenty-one stories, 1,020 rooms and a hundred suites. Since opening its doors in 1958, the Queen E, as it's known locally, has accommodated more than 22 million travellers, including royalty, statesmen and luminary stars of movies, sports and rock. The 1976 Olympic Games were headquartered under this roof and a few years prior to that, as humanity set off to walk on the moon for the very first time, another universal event took place at the hotel.

John Lennon and Yoko Ono bedded down for a week at the Queen Elizabeth in 1969, papering the windows of their suite, rooms 1738–1742, with handmade posters. The hirsute Beatle held court with the likes of Rabbi Abraham Feinberg of Toronto, and a phrase that came out of that meeting hung in the air like a possible dream: *Give peace a chance*. On the night of June 1, about forty people with a potluck assortment of guitars, tambourines and noisemakers packed the hotel room. With tape rolling and Lennon on lead vocals, this rag-gle-taggle band of journalists, celebrities, friends and at least one hotel employee made musical history and gave the world one of its most endearing songs. Almost every December 8, since Lennon's death in 1980, someone (the hotel staff claims not to know who) has left two dozen roses — twelve white and twelve red — at the door of the room.

The entertainment in my room of the Queen E, however, didn't quite make that league. The TV had thirty channels — eleven English and nineteen French — and not one of them held my attention for more than a minute. Around half-past

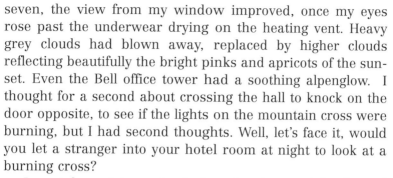

seven, the view from my window improved, once my eyes rose past the underwear drying on the heating vent. Heavy grey clouds had blown away, replaced by higher clouds reflecting beautifully the bright pinks and apricots of the sunset. Even the Bell office tower had a soothing alpenglow. I thought for a second about crossing the hall to knock on the door opposite, to see if the lights on the mountain cross were burning, but I had second thoughts. Well, let's face it, would you let a stranger into your hotel room at night to look at a burning cross?

I went downstairs and poked my head around the door of Le Montréalais Bistro Bar Restaurant, a place that I soon decided could do without the likes of my faded blue jeans toning down its ambience. I then checked out the fabled Beaver Club at the other end of the lobby, marked by a vintage sign with four brass bells hung beneath it. Founded by early fur traders and pioneer entrepreneurs, this elite club registers more than nine hundred members throughout the world, including kings, queens and heads of state. The cuisine is said to be among the best in the province, with a far-reaching wine selection to match. I smiled at the stuffed beaver that guarded the entrance and chose to cast my culinary net and modest budget further afield. I stepped out into the evening and onto the sidewalk of René-Lévesque Boulevard.

Montreal has many things to offer a visitor, if the visitor lives long enough to enjoy them. I'm talking about traffic here, and it's far safer talking about it than being part of it. My mother always said that if I couldn't say something nice about people, including Montreal's drivers, I shouldn't say anything at all. So I won't.

There is a coping mechanism for Montreal traffic, however: underground walkways and corridors. Dozens of them lead from office towers to shopping malls, from train stations to hotels, and back again. It began in 1962 with the building of Place Ville Marie and now is the largest subterranean network of its kind in the world. You can walk for miles and miles down there, protected from the oppressive heat of summer, the blizzards of winter, and the motorists of all year long. I went down to roam the city's labyrinth of a basement and an hour later, after much window-shopping and doorway menu-browsing, found myself in Les Halles de la Gare. At least I'd saved the cab fare home.

Most of the stores and cafés cater to the daytime office crowds and were closed that evening, but one or two remained open, including a bar named The Planet. A noisy karaoke party writhed and moaned in the room next door, with a tragic lack of talent available to end its misery. I took a seat at the bar and after saying hello in French I ordered in English: a chicken sandwich, fries and a green salad to go, and a glass of red wine to stay, while I waited for my food. My Quebec City dining experience led me to suspect I'd have enough time to drink my wine, replenish it, finish reading my two-hundred-page book and have a useful nap. So imagine my pleasant surprise when the waiter brought my packaged meal five minutes later. I was even more surprised when the barmaid generously offered to break a few liquor laws and pour my wine, which I'd barely sipped, into a takeout coffee cup with a tight lid, so I could take it back to my room as well. What on earth would Monsieur Richardson say about *that* if he knew?

The next morning I walked a couple of blocks to the old CPR headquarters and station. The traffic wasn't really that bad and most of it stayed completely off the sidewalk and left me alone. Windsor Station, at Rue de la Gauchitière and Peel, stands like a castle, wedged firmly into a hillside of the city. Built in 1888, it was expanded and renovated many times over the years, including the addition of a remarkable glass-roofed concourse, installed somewhat ahead of its time in 1913. Bruce Price, the American architect who designed the Château Frontenac, also designed this building. In the 1890s he designed a few New York skyscrapers with heavy Renaissance detail, described by one critic as "without disci-pline...hearty, violent and free," and also gave a new look to summer hotel and cottage architecture. Price loved the round towers he'd seen in the Loire Valley, and he worked their essence into several recreational properties and hotels on the East Coast. His best work, according to those who profess to know such things, appeared in cottages he designed in 1885 for Tuxedo Park, New York. Those same people say Windsor Station is somewhat Richardsonian, after architect H.H. Richardson. The former platform, peaceful and clean as a new pin, belies the screaming of steel wheels, hissing steam and coal dust that once filled its air. On November 6, 1960, the last CPR steam train chugged into Windsor Station, completing its final run for the company and ending an era.

Though the place is not exactly a museum, there were artifacts and displays to amuse the casual railway buff. A circular waiting room bench, beautifully crafted, and a magnificent station clock caught and held my attention. With its vault-like lower levels, the station provides a fitting home for, among other services, the national CP archives. For the price of making an appointment, which I had done, one can gain access to the inner sanctum of the archives. The rest of my day in Montreal, amid thousands of old railway photographs, brochures, timetables, maps, posters and glorious assorted memorabilia, was soon spent, and most enjoyably.

Montreal
~to~
Ottawa

AFTER SEEING THE LAST SPIKE DRIVEN INTO CANADA'S FIRST transcontinental railway, on a cold and cloudy November 7, 1885, William Van Horne boasted that the trip from Montreal to Vancouver would now take only eighty-five hours. He was optimistic. The journey took almost a week, depending on weather and mechanical breakdowns, but even that was impressive for the period.

The first through freight train from Montreal arrived at the western terminus of Port Moody on November 22, 1885, carrying several hundred barrels of oil destined for the navy at the Esquimalt docks on Vancouver Island. "The naval supplies," noted Victoria's *Daily Colonist,* "have reached Esquimalt in seven days [actually six days, eleven hours], or fifteen days from England, a fact that must be hailed with delight by Englishmen and Canadians. It will also be a startling fact to other European powers, for it proves to them that troops and munitions of war can be landed on the chief Pacific station of the British navy in a little over two weeks time." While the CPR appeared to its funding government as a crucial link between central and western Canada, and a vital component of imperial defence, it wasn't long before tourism climbed aboard for the ride.

Fourteen years later, in 1899, the CPR launched *The Imperial Limited*, a passenger train service that steamed from Montreal to Vancouver at an average speed of twenty-nine miles per hour. This reduced cross-country travel time to about one hundred hours and could deliver Orient-bound passengers to the CP Empress ships docked in Vancouver: the *Empress of India*, the *Empress of China* and the *Empress of Japan*. Despite competition from eighteen other shipping companies, these vessels dominated the lucrative North Pacific passenger line of that era, carrying 60 percent of all traffic.

In 1931, a Royal Commission looked into the competition between CPR and CNR, which led to the pooling of passengers between Montreal and Toronto. By 1932, passenger business was so bad that CPR suspended its dividends. On June 28, 1936, however, one hundred years after the first passenger train ran in this country, a special fiftieth-anniversary Hudson-type locomotive, No. 2803, left Montreal to cross the country, amid much pomp and circumstance. In August, 1944, a restored locomotive, No. 374, steamed out of CP's Montreal shops to make one final run across Canada to Vancouver, where it became a static display in a city park.

Though still enjoying a glorious place in the hearts of all those who knew them, imbuing staff, passengers and onlookers with a romantic sense of travel, steam trains were slowly heading out for good. In March, 1949, CPR took delivery of its last new steam locomotive from Montreal Locomotive Works, No. 5935, and bought its first diesel-electric locomotives six months later.

I left Montreal station on Saturday morning at 10:17 a.m., on VIA train No. 33, pulled by locomotive No. 6413. I travelled economy class, sharing a seventy-two-seat car with about twenty other passengers. My fellow travellers were a cheerful, talkative bunch, mostly younger people, many with backpacks. After eight days of journeying I'd already noticed a difference in train ambience between weekday and weekend trips. As we got underway, a bilingual taped announcement informed us of the safety features, and an attendant demonstrated the familiar window-breaking escape routine to those sitting near emergency exits.

We trundled along at a jogger's pace, passing through a freight yard of several hundred acres, where long lines of rail cars waited with colourful loads of new automobiles and pickup trucks, glinting in the bright sunshine. The next freight train we passed was readying to leave with thousands of new telephone poles, destined, I thought, to replace those damaged by the major ice storm that hit this region a few years ago.

The train zipped past Lachine Station at a fair clip but slowed to a halt at Dorval two minutes later to pick up a few passengers. The city sprawled away to my right, and it was easy to forget that I was looking at an island. Perhaps not a *real* island, as some coastal Canadians might argue, but a couple of rivers do surround it with water. About twenty minutes after leaving Gare Centrale we crossed a bridge and left Montreal, only to stop by a cornfield moments later for no apparent reason. All was very quiet, then a VIA train flashed past in the opposite direction at amazing speed. A whooshing blur, gone. I could see why train wrecks might be quite spectacular, and why little hammers wouldn't always be required to break windows.

At eleven-thirty, the smart red brick station of Alexandra marked our halfway point, approximately, and by noon the train howled non-stop as we crossed road after road. We pulled into Ottawa Station about ten minutes behind schedule.

The airy, street-level platforms were flooded with bright sunlight that fell between the long, thin steel roofs. Steps descended to a tiled subway that led beneath the tracks and connected to a ramp that circled back up and into the main hall of the station, a bright space held together by modern girders and lots of glass. Apart from the twenty or so people who had got off my train, the place was fairly quiet. One or two went straight to the central ticketing counter and a few others made for a bank of pay phones by the wall. I paused on my way to the exit to look at four model trains displayed in glass cases, representing different eras of rail travel in the area. Along with the *Ottawa*, which ran on the Ottawa and

Prescott Railway from around 1854, there were three less distinctive locomotives from 1927, 1944 and 1948.

At the doorway I looked for the familiar landmarks of the nation's capital — the stately Peace Tower rising high above the seat of federal government, and the steep green roof of the grand Château Laurier Hotel, my home for the next twenty-four hours. But the train station is on Tremblay Road, out in the suburbs. Downtown was still some kind of ride away.

Getting out of the taxi at the front door of the Château Laurier, I could see that the hotel used to be much handier for the train. I stood and gazed from beneath the five-arch porte-cochère, two cars wide and four cars long, at the main entrance. Right across the street stood the old station, stately and solid, now employed as a conference centre.

I should introduce Charles Melville Hayes at this point, the man responsible for both buildings. He was a forceful, flamboyant man of action and, according to a few of his peers, an occasional scoundrel — in short, a typical railway baron of the post-Victorian era and a good fit for the presidency of the Grand Trunk Railway, which he acquired in 1909 after serving as its general manager for twelve years. As the nation's railway system expanded, so did the hordes that wanted to travel further afield and see new sights. This feisty American was brought in to steer those hordes — and their money — in the right direction.

He built a first-rate train station and a neighbouring hotel on prime land alongside the Rideau Canal, sparing little expense. Ross and MacFarlane of Montreal handled the architecture, and construction of the CPR trademark Château-style railway hotel began late in 1907. The founders would name the hotel in honour of Canada's eighth prime minister, the Liberal Wilfrid Laurier, first elected in 1896 and not defeated until 1911. Laurier initially disliked the idea but eventually gave his consent.

In the spring of 1912, with completion just weeks away, Hayes collected lavish European furnishings for the hotel and booked passage for them, himself and his family aboard a luxury steamship leaving Southampton in April that year. The ship was the *Titanic*, which took the Château Laurier's furniture to the bottom of the Atlantic. Hayes and his family managed to get into a lifeboat but he perished. His body lies buried in Montreal.

At eleven o'clock Eastern Time on the morning of April 25, eleven days after the tragedy at sea, the entire Grand Trunk rail system across Canada and the United States came to a halt, in silent tribute to its lost president. It was out of continued respect for Charles Melville Hayes that on June 1, 1912, the Château Laurier set a precedent by being the only hotel of such grandeur to open without a formal ceremony. The press, I should report, did partake of complimentary food and drink that evening, courtesy of the hotel's manager.

Naturally, Sir Wilfrid Laurier put the first signature in the hotel guest book, but he wasn't as thrilled as he might have been. A bust made in his honour and displayed proudly in the hotel lobby had been dropped by workmen and repaired with a somewhat larger, more crooked nose.

The hotel had barely established a name for itself when the First World War made crossing the Atlantic a most unattractive proposition for the rich and famous Europeans who accounted for much of the clientele. The Laurier survived those lean years and made up for them during the radio boom of the 1920s, when live music from the ballroom filled the airwaves. (Canada's public broadcast service, the CBC, still occupies a studio in the building.) Popularity forced an expansion in 1929 and 250 rooms were added.

When the railways were nationalized in the 1920s, the Grand Trunk became part of CN, which administered the hotel until it was sold to CP in 1988.

I entered the lobby and was immediately impressed by its high, plaster relief ceiling decorated with a recurring bunch of

Graceful curves are a hallmark of this urban hotel.
Photo: Dave Preston

grapes, immaculate oak panelling along the walls, and tan marble floor with a lustre deep enough to lose your baggage in. The front desk and its heavy marble counter were fully employed so I strolled around, soaking up the luxury and comparing it, favourably but not exceedingly, to the Château Frontenac.

The beaky bust of Laurier was nowhere to be seen, but a life-size bronze sculpture, *Mother and Child* by Lea Vivot, sat boldly between two pillars of the lobby. The Canadian Machine Gun Corps formed at the hotel in August, 1914, and a bronze plaque commemorates it and salutes those of its number who died in the First World War. Standing proudly as it does in the nation's capital, the hotel has garnered a host of military connections and memories. In May 1939, George VI and Queen Elizabeth arrived by carriage to dedicate a war memorial. When the Second World War broke out a few months later, statesmen, dignitaries and generals poured into the city, many of them staying at the Château Laurier. In 1946 Winston Churchill made an historic TV broadcast from his suite in the hotel. Guests such as these made use of a private entrance, and certain rooms, such as No. 458, looked quite ordinary from the hallway but concealed huge, opulent suites within.

Approaching the lounge I found another oak-panelled room, a permanent display area for portraits taken by the world-famous Canadian photographer Yousef Karsh. He kept a studio in the Château Laurier from 1973 to 1992 and lived with his wife in the hotel for eighteen years, until 1998. The portraits I saw included the famous one of a scowling Winston Churchill (taken in 1941, when Karsh snatched the trademark cigar from Churchill's mouth and quickly snapped the picture), Albert Einstein (1948) and Pablo Casals (1954). Each shows a timeless form and clarity that Karsh captured like no other photographer before or since.

Check-in completed, I went with a bellboy who insisted on carrying my luggage aboard his big brassy cart to my room on the second floor. The dark mahogany doors with brass numbers are original, and the colour of good chocolate. My suite had a king-sized bed, a long couch, tall armoire and bar with TV; a wall divided the bedroom from a space with a desk and large closet. The walls glowed warmly in shades of pale pink,

The Château Laurier's subterranean pool has remained almost the same for more than fifty years. Photo: Château Laurier

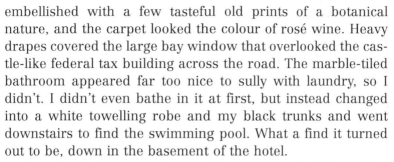

embellished with a few tasteful old prints of a botanical nature, and the carpet looked the colour of rosé wine. Heavy drapes covered the large bay window that overlooked the castle-like federal tax building across the road. The marble-tiled bathroom appeared far too nice to sully with laundry, so I didn't. I didn't even bathe in it at first, but instead changed into a white towelling robe and my black trunks and went downstairs to find the swimming pool. What a find it turned out to be, down in the basement of the hotel.

An attendant behind the counter gave me a brilliant white towel and I stepped through a heavy door into a bygone afternoon. The Laurier's pool reeks of nostalgia. Handsomely tiled, with heavy brass rails and wrought-iron work, I could not have picked a more lovely setting for a cool dip. No natural light reaches this alluring, subterranean cavern, but along one side of the pool's apron sits a row of lounging chairs with large copper lamps mounted on the wall to supply reading light. A large marble alcove stands at one end of the pool, having housed a statue at some time I suppose, but now the lush green tendrils of a small ivy plant cling there.

A spectator's gallery runs around the upper level, furnished with comfortable chairs and tables draped in crisp white linen. How I longed for a few pool party friends to drop by for cocktails and idle banter, and perhaps a crustless cucumber sandwich…but I contented myself with a quiet, dusky swim.

The changing rooms next door, His and Hers, still hold the original oak doors, wooden benches and partitions, and thickly marbled walls. A masseuse could knead and rub me for $60 an hour, but I had plans to spend that time, and some of that money, on dinner. I changed in my room and went back downstairs to find a meal.

Just off the lobby, the entrance to Wilfrid's, the hotel restaurant, caught my eye. I browsed the tall menu, tempted by the offerings and the price, but late afternoon sun beckoned me further afield and I headed for the outdoors. I came across two bridal parties, one using the ballroom downstairs and another on the terrace above the canal, with a capital view of Parliament Hill and a warm breeze that billowed white chiffon like a photographer's dream.

I took the steps down to the edge of the canal, now covered by cool, early evening shade. Built by Irish labourers and British troops between 1826 and 1832, the waterway gave locals a sneaky route to Lake Ontario in the event that cantankerous Americans had tied up the St. Lawrence River to the northeast. The region's earliest railway, or tramway I suppose, was built here in 1827. It brought quarried stone from a place called Hog's Back almost a mile away, for use in the canal's locks and weirs. After the canal opened the railway was scrapped.

Forty-six hand-operated locks, eight of them quite close to the hotel, open and close frequently during summer to let recreational boaters get from Kingston to Montreal. In winter the canal becomes the world's longest ice rink, with about five miles of it groomed for use by pleasure skaters and the

occasional commuter. The Rideau Canal is a National Historic Site and accounts for almost a million visitors every year, though how they do this accounting I really can't imagine.

Having roamed a fine-looking downtown, I sat on a thick stone wall by Parliament Hill and watched thousands of tourists arrive by bus,

The Château Laurier presides over Rideau Canal locks.
Photo: Dave Preston

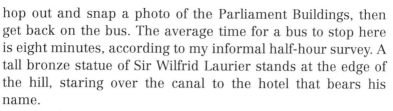

hop out and snap a photo of the Parliament Buildings, then get back on the bus. The average time for a bus to stop here is eight minutes, according to my informal half-hour survey. A tall bronze statue of Sir Wilfrid Laurier stands at the edge of the hill, staring over the canal to the hotel that bears his name.

I decided that a fitting place to eat that evening was D'Arcy McGee's pub. D'Arcy Magee, an outspoken Irish journalist and member of the "Young Ireland" movement who sought refuge in America, became the first (and only, so far) Canadian politician to be assassinated. A member of the Fenian Brotherhood gunned him down on April 7, 1868, as he walked along Sparks Street just yards from where the pub now stands. I raised a glass of Irish ale to his memory's health, and downed a plate of fish and chips to my own.

Parliament Hill by night appeared just as handsome as it did by day. Floodlights gave the towering stone buildings a mature, weathered texture, and I strolled back through warm night air, crossing a fathomless black canal to my grand Château. Entering the hotel by the front lobby I caught sight of the indoor wedding party in full, boisterous swing. I had half a mind to slip into the room and join them, but instead went up to my own room and slipped into a very large, very soft bed.

The room was incredibly quiet and dark when the drapes were drawn. It was hard to believe I was in downtown any-where, and it made sleeping late on Sunday morning quite an easy task. If it's ever my lot to be laid out in a chapel of rest, something like this would do nicely.

Sometime before noon, I made my way back outside and took the air, as a few others were doing, in Major Hill's park behind the hotel. Originally the home of Colonel John By, after whom the original settlement was named Bytown, the site became the city's first official park on July 1, 1867, with 101 guns booming a salute.

Years earlier, on Christmas Day, 1854, the Bytown and

Prescott Railway opened, bringing the first rail traffic from fifty-four miles out of town. Officials renamed the city Ottawa the following year, and the service became the Ottawa and Prescott Railway Company before being taken over by CP. This seemed a good opportunity to sit a while and think a bit about railway gauges.

The standard railway track gauge of 4 feet 8 1/2 inches was fixed by an act of British parliament in 1840 and has been attributed to an English chap named William Jessop. (Though we can also accuse the Romans. Tramways built in early British coal mines were the same width as a common road wagon, which had acquired its own standard width from the Roman chariots, based out of necessity on the span of two horse backsides.) The grandfather of steam locomotion, George Stephenson, was an advocate of the standard gauge, although various railways had their own special widths.

In North America, as many as twenty-five different gauges were in use during the first part of the nineteenth century. On July 31, 1851, Ontario and Quebec adopted the 5 1/2-foot "broad" gauge and it remained in use until about 1870, after which a gradual change to the current 4-foot 8 1/2-inch standard gauge crept into use. In 1910, the last remaining broad gauge line in North America, the Carillon and Grenville Railway, was abandoned. It was bought a year later by the Canadian Northern Railway as part of its new Montreal to Ottawa line. Prince Edward Island continued to use narrower tracks until 1930, when the final section changed to standard gauge. In 1949, Newfoundland became the tenth province of Canada and the Newfoundland Railway and its narrow gauge track became part of the Canadian National system. That, too, soon went the way of most non-conformists in a federal system.

And by my gauge that was enough time to sit and think on a fine Sunday afternoon in Ottawa, especially when there were bags to pack and a train to catch.

Ottawa
~to~
Toronto

ONCE UPON A TIME — AND CANADIANS ACROSS THE LAND MIGHT argue exactly when that time was — *everyone* knew their local train station inside out. The station was often the first thing to be built in a settling community. The streets radiated from it and the town grew up around it. The station held rank with the town hall and no one had to walk far in any direction before they came upon a sign pointing them back to it. Indeed, the tracks often marked a critical boundary that divided a town into distinct neighbourhoods and segregated the social classes. Regardless of topography or points of a compass, the tracks almost always had a wrong side on which to live. For generations, the station served as the main portal to a town, a traveller's first impression and a logical base for ancillary transportation. Many had adjoining stables, followed by cab companies, car rental offices and bus depots. You might have had a problem directing strangers to the opera house or the Catholic church or the best restaurant in town, but you could have been blindfolded and still led them to the train station. Sadly, this was once upon a time.

Although he certainly knew where it used to be, the cab driver who picked me up outside the Chateau Laurier did not know, for sure, where to find the Ottawa train station. So I told him and we arrived there within fifteen minutes.

A good half-hour stretched between me and the No. 49 train to Toronto, so I thought I'd spend some of it in the

Panorama Lounge. This cosy gathering place for those fortunate enough to be travelling first class spoils you with free non-alcoholic beverages and reading materials, away from the hoi-polloi of the station's main hall. After putting my luggage onto the cart by the door, I helped myself to a tomato juice from the tiny kitchen bar, picked up a magazine and sat next to a young mother and her lively preschool son. We talked a while and exchanged many smiles but she privately wished, I think, that she were at home, where tomato juice stains are so much easier to remove.

Ten minutes before train time, a redcap politely asked us to take the elevator down a floor and walk through the tunnel to Track 2, while he took our luggage along a different route. The redcap's job must be easier than it used to be, and they don't seem to wear red caps any more. Trendy red golf shirts with navy trim and the VIA insignia make up the uniform, and hotel-style baggage carts have brought a touch of class to the operation, not to mention a step toward gender equality. Throughout the world for more than a century, porting luggage around a railway station was an exclusively male domain (as was building, fuelling, conducting and driving all the trains). When CN hired only its second woman for the job, she worked right here at Union Station in Ottawa. Susan Proux, a petite five-feet-two and a shade over a hundred pounds, turned passenger heads as she carried heavy bags and baggage around the place. "Since I can and it's not hurting me, why shouldn't I?" she told one reporter. A man once gave her a dollar tip before she picked up his bags, then another as she delivered them safely to his car, saying, "I still don't believe it." The sisterhood failed to show unanimous support, though, and a woman passenger scolded her, saying, "You're lowering yourself by doing this kind of work. I don't think it's right for you to be among all these men." But that was way back in the dark ages of 1976.

For the third time in a week, I had the same seat in the VIA 1 section, so I almost gave the window-breaking demonstration myself. On this occasion, however, I had a seatmate.

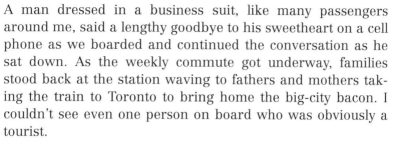

A man dressed in a business suit, like many passengers around me, said a lengthy goodbye to his sweetheart on a cell phone as we boarded and continued the conversation as he sat down. As the weekly commute got underway, families stood back at the station waving to fathers and mothers taking the train to Toronto to bring home the big-city bacon. I couldn't see even one person on board who was obviously a tourist.

The train rolled out on time and I watched a chunky parade of apartment buildings go by, many of them with plastic grocery bags and empty milk jugs strung around the balcony to deter birds. The effect was shabbily festive, and it seemed to work. I didn't see a feathered creature anywhere.

I scribbled in my notepad as we left the suburbs and the industrial areas of Ottawa and made our way smoothly into Ontario farmland and muskeg. The sun lowered to an angle that cut through and across the carriage so I put on sunglasses, rather than pull the drapes across and lose the view over the fields and woodland. Some of the telephone poles that ran for mile after mile alongside the track stood neglected, their sad, slack lines smothered by creepers and encroaching bush. Sleep came easily to many passengers as the train developed a slow, occasional roll. It felt much like being on board a ship. Minutes melted one into another, marked only by a lazy, slow-fading sunset that lulled all aboard into a peaceful reverie.

Perhaps afraid that we might drift away and miss the essence of the ride, an attendant came around to hand out hot lemony face-cloths to wake and freshen us, so hot that he warned each of us to be careful. The hot wipe that refreshes certainly worked, alerting me once again to all that swept before and past me.

My seatmate and I shared a comfortable silence for a few miles, but we introduced ourselves over a delicious little dinner. We both chose the Atlantic salmon, as opposed to lasagna or chicken. The appetizer was smoked salmon on bread with a piquant sauce, which he obviously enjoyed and took to be the main course, as he then tucked into the pecan pie served on the tray at the same time. So, with his dessert finished and his mouth wiped, he sheepishly retrieved his cutlery from the debris on his tray and ate the salmon entrée when it arrived. I suppressed a giggle for a moment, then buried it as quietly as I could in my napkin.

Mark lived in Ottawa and was heading to Belleville to learn something marvellous about a piece of software. It had something to do with servers and computer networks, and although I spent more than a dozen years in that industry I find it hard to stay awake for more than five minutes' talk of it now. He made this trip less often than some of the other regular passengers, but he'd become so familiar with the route he barely looked out the window and, unlike me, never wondered aloud where we were.

Another man across the aisle played solitaire on his laptop computer while speaking into a cell phone. He seemed quite adept at both activities, though fully engaged in neither one, and showed a certain stamina for it that must only come after years of practice. One or two others within my view flipped idly through large three-ring binders, and a young woman held a paperback novel close to her chest and looked out into the darkening evening, as if she daren't read the next line.

The Ottawa–Toronto rail service received 35 million dollars in the 1980s to make it run faster. Prior to this boost, the train often slowed to a leisurely forty miles per hour between Ottawa and Brockville — a bit too leisurely for the likes of most workaday folk. Although total traffic along this route had increased by almost half, there was only a 16 percent increase in railway ridership for the same period. Time is money to business travellers, and airlines proved to be a wiser investment of it. However, track improvements allowed these trains to reach ninety-five miles per hour, the same speed they ran on the Brockville–Toronto leg of the route. By shaving an hour off the travel time, the number of passengers increased dramatically from about 220,000 to more than 300,000 a year. VIA has apparently worked hard to compete

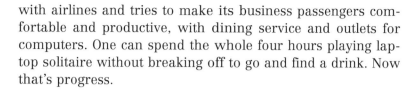

with airlines and tries to make its business passengers comfortable and productive, with dining service and outlets for computers. One can spend the whole four hours playing laptop solitaire without breaking off to go and find a drink. Now that's progress.

The train's first stop saw us at the red brick station of Smith Falls, where we met the Ottawa-bound train, looking remarkably similar to ours and laden with people who I'm sure live in one place but must occasionally go to work in another. We pulled away and gathered speed, only to slow once again to cross a small bridge over a canal. I noticed a lone kayaker pitching a small orange tent and preparing for a grassy night by the water, like some contemporary voyageur. The lingering sunset, one of the most tenacious I've ever seen, hung beautifully in the sky behind him, with a custard-yellow half-moon rising in the southeast. I was definitely on the right side of the train to enjoy this ride. My seatmate, meanwhile, had become more enamoured of the bar cart, as had many other seasoned travellers of this line. They seemed to engage in a collective numbing of pain at this sombre launch of another week away from home.

I rarely use the phrase "Of course, I'm too young to remember," though I'm certainly reaching an age where it could become a routine opening for many an observation. The fact is, I don't remember the old-fashioned saloon bar cars or dining rooms on a train. I did enjoy the dining car and bar on the Maritimes leg of my journey and was looking forward to similar fun as I crossed the country, from Toronto to Vancouver, on *The Canadian*. But the bar cart and meal-on-a-tray system used on this commuter corridor — ideas garnered from the airline industry — encourage, if not enforce, passengers to remain seated, removing an opportunity to make new friends among fellow travellers and perhaps compare travel notes. Sitting down at a table for four in a dining car, or standing elbow to cordial elbow in a bar car, are surely much more conducive to a warm social atmosphere and happy passengers. I realize, of course, that space on a commuter train is tight, though not as tight as it is on aircraft, but until the day we're travelling so fast that air turbulence becomes a danger factor for the train I would like to get up and walk around a bit. Especially on trips lasting more than a couple of hours. I'll leave it at that, before I put on my Bing Crosby voice and break into a rousing chorus of "Don't Fence Me In."

We stopped to unload a few souls at Brockville, where, on New Year's Eve in 1860, the Brockville and Ottawa Railway opened the first railway tunnel in Canada, one that ran for a third of a mile under the town. We stopped a while later to listen to a recurring announcement telling us the train was waiting for a signal. By the time it came and we reached Kingston, the night was tunnel black.

Mark left me at Belleville with a firm handshake and a wish of good luck, and I reclined my seat for a nap. Throughout the car, no one spoke. It was like travelling in a horizontal elevator but much easier to avoid eye contact. I heard the tinny simmering of someone's headphones and tried to identify the tune, only to doze off before the second chorus. Waking moments before we pulled into Toronto's Union Station, I joined the rest of the carriage in a loosely choreographed stretching, yawning, scratching dance.

Just one other train stood on the tracks of the station at this hour, and the passengers disembarked with a routine disinterest. I was the last off, as usual, having toyed with the idea of breaking the window with a little hammer and finally letting my humble seat cushion play its vital role in saving my life. At least I had a clear run at the empty corridor with my luggage, which seemed to get heavier and more bulky at every stop. I followed the herd along the subterranean hallway into the main station, but the others quickly disappeared outside into the sodium glare of the city. Union Station is the busiest depot in Canada, handling more than 24 million passengers a year, but on this late Sunday evening they'd all left me alone, in relative calm and desolation. I felt like an elderly parishioner who'd missed the church service but could still enjoy the majestic ambience of an empty cathedral. I would return — I had to — in better light and with more energy to explore this place. After a few moments my gaze caught the sign to the old passageway that leads under Front Street and across to the Royal York. Never is such a connection, linking station to hotel, more welcome to a traveller than late at night.

Please indulge me while I tell you a short story. A guest is staying at a hotel and must be up in time for a meeting the next day, so he requests a wake-up call. In the morning there's a knock at the door and a nervous bellboy says "Excuse me sir, but was your wake-up call for seven-thirty or eight-thirty?"

Toronto's Union Station was built like a cathedral, according to Edward, Prince of Wales, when he opened it in 1927.
Photo: Dave Preston

"Seven-thirty," replies the guest, "and what time is it now?"

"Er, nine-fifteen," says the bellboy.

Sadly for some, the days of the early morning wake-up call are numbered. Over the years I have been roused from sleep by hotel employees tapping at my door and by phone calls made from the front desk by real live people, with whom I could have a short conversation about the weather, breakfast,

Toronto's Royal York, the "city within a city block" once had its own golf course, just a carriage ride away.
Photo: The Royal York Hotel

or my chances of making a nine o'clock flight. Then came the automated phone call: the precise call that woke me up on time but often let me begin the day feeling more stupid than usual, as I answered the phone politely and tried to speak to a recorded voice.

Although still available in most hotels, the wake-up phone call has been all but replaced by the radio alarm clock, or, in some extravagant cases, by the CD/tapedeck/radio alarm clock. And so it was that in the dense, grey dawning hours of Monday, when I, like Chuck Berry, had No Particular Place to Go, I was shocked out of a blissful dream by shrieking voices from the side of my bed. The radio alarm had somehow been set for 6:00 a.m. and tuned to bring in what appeared to be live reports from a wailing banshee conference. I gradually recognized the room that lurched and swayed into focus as the one I had wearily checked into the previous night, on the second floor of the Royal York Hotel. Now let me be clear, I am certainly not accusing the hotel staff of leaving the alarm set to go off, but I am accusing a certain radio alarm clock manufacturer of failing to make its gadget more simple to program. I distinctly recall asking for easy listening music, no sooner than 8:00 a.m. But here I was, wide awake at a minute past six, so rather than waste a good chunk of the morning I promptly went back to sleep.

Let me begin again, much further back — before the Royal York Hotel and before the city of Toronto. In 1843, an accomplished sailor of the Great Lakes, Captain Thomas Dick, built himself four brick terrace houses on Front Street in the lakeside town of York, the capital of Upper Canada. The terrace grew into a row and housed the Knox Theological College, before being renovated and renamed Sword's Hotel in 1853. When the capital of Upper Canada moved to Quebec City in 1857, Sword's Hotel changed hands and became Revere House. It kept this name for five years until the return of Captain Dick, who gave the place two new wings, a facelift and another new name: Queen's Hotel. Four hundred guests could enjoy stylish accommodation at Queen's, where Prime Minister Sir John A. Macdonald supposedly met with plotting sympathizers of the American Civil War. Boomtown exploded all around it, and the hotel enjoyed many renovations and expansions during its notable career. It was the first hotel in Canada to use a hot-air furnace for heating and the first to install a business telephone and a passenger elevator. It was also the first hotel to pipe water to its rooms, a feature that proved to be more than just convenient. A fire swept across downtown Toronto in April, 1904, and staff, guests and passersby saved the hotel by using blankets soaked in bath-tubs filled with water. As the blaze, whipped by a fierce wind, burned its way through fourteen acres of the city, firefighters came by train from as far away as Buffalo.

As big and as grand, and, indeed, as lucky as it was, a demolition crew removed the Queen's in 1927, amid loud local protest, to make way for something better.

Encouraged by the success of the Château Frontenac in Quebec, the CPR began scheming to create the largest hotel in the British Commonwealth. A chain of luxury CPR hotels stretched across the country, from The Algonquin on the east coast to The Empress on the west, and the Roaring Twenties brought roaring success to each of them. However, the golden chain was missing a vital and lucrative link in Toronto. (It also required a link in Saskatchewan, the only province without a major railway hotel. In 1926, work began on the Hotel Saskatchewan in Regina and CP returned its focus to Toronto.)

As soon as workers cleared the 75,000-square-foot lot, construction began. Although CPR executives "searched the globe for designs and ideas," and most certainly examined New York and Chicago, the Royal York became one of the first such projects to use purely Canadian expertise. CPR's favourite architectural firm of Edward and W.S. Maxwell lost a senior partner when Edward died in 1923, so Ross and McDonald of Montreal won the contract, working in conjunc-

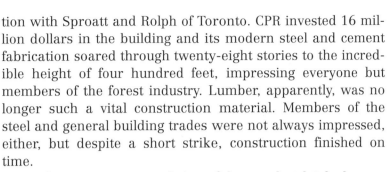

tion with Sproatt and Rolph of Toronto. CPR invested 16 million dollars in the building and its modern steel and cement fabrication soared through twenty-eight stories to the incredible height of four hundred feet, impressing everyone but members of the forest industry. Lumber, apparently, was no longer such a vital construction material. Members of the steel and general building trades were not always impressed, either, but despite a short strike, construction finished on time.

As the minutes to completion of the new hotel ticked away, the boasting grew loud enough to be heard around the globe. Behind the scenes, the hotel would have its own water works; a self-contained power plant; a telephone system requiring thirty-five operators; a radio station that could broadcast to trains and to steamships on Lake Ontario and the St. Lawrence; a silver-plating plant built into the roof, to maintain the 84,000 pieces of flatware; and a laundry that could handle 160,000 articles of linen. Coal, the dirty bane of solid fuel heating, was nowhere to be seen or smelled, as pressurized steam was piped from almost a mile away.

Ten ornate passenger elevators led to 1,048 rooms, every one of them with a radio, private shower and tub. About seven thousand miles of carpeting cushioned the hallways and floors. The hotel had its own private hospital with a dozen beds in two wards, an operating theatre, dispensary and separate waiting rooms for guests and staff; a library containing more than twelve thousand books; a grand concert hall with a full stage and the largest pipe organ in Canada — a melodious monster weighing fifty tons and containing enough copper wire to reach Ottawa. Add to this package the country's largest bakery, a small "police" and fire department, a bank, stores, restaurants, shops, hairdressers and a newspaper plant, and its claim of being "a city within a city block" becomes credible. The hotel even had its own golf course (now the St. George Golf and Country Club), a few miles to the west in Etobicoke, and delivered guests to the clubhouse by carriage.

A hotel radio personality kept guests, trains and steamships informed. Photo: The Royal York Hotel

On Tuesday, June 11, 1929, the Royal York doors opened. CPR president at the time, Edward W. Beatty, included the following remarks in his opening address:

> The years that have passed since the first train reached this city from Montreal, forty-five in all, have been years marked by great progress in the city. In 1928 ...the [local] net earnings of the Canadian Pacific were in excess of $64,000,000. These figures are indicative, not only of the fact that Toronto has progressed, but of the fact that Canada has made substantial progress, because its progress is inevitably reflected in railway earnings.

Beatty, a former lawyer, spent all his life as a bachelor and spent all his love on the CP railroad, fighting hard to keep it a private corporation.

Viscount Wellington, the Governor General of Canada, formally opened the Royal York on June 29, 1929: "To provide the hospitality and good cheer for which Toronto has ever been noted." Four simultaneous gala balls filled the tallest building in the British Empire with raucous cheer that night, a room cost two dollars, and everyone was suitably impressed. *Construction* magazine called it "a veritable poem in stone" possibly referring to the massive granite plinth on which it sat and the Indiana limestone that faced the entire building. Front Street, with its towering new hotel and Union Station dead opposite, now looked like a fashionable section of New York's Seventh Avenue. King George VI visited the first year, as did Winston Churchill. Business came easily and an extension added 160 rooms within twelve months of opening. For thirty years, the largest hotel in Canada would be the Royal York.

Barely had the streamers and bunting been cleared away when the Depression took most of the guests with it. Struggling to survive the early 1930s, the hotel drafted top entertainers, such as Al Jolson, to boost occupancy rates.

I set out to explore the Royal York with Tom, an employee, as my guide. We toured the public areas and took an inquisitive look behind the scenes, much as novelist Arthur Hailey did when he lived in the building for a while, gathering material for his book *Hotel*. After lengthy walks along a maze of basement passages and hallways, frequently stepping aside so as not to impede the endless procession of laundry carts and various supplies, we turned into a corridor known by employees as Info Alley that led to the staff cafeteria. Photos old and new of staff and guests, souvenir menus and numerous awards almost covered the wall. Tom's an avid historian and, like me, something of an archivist — or pack rat, as most tidy people of the tidy world tend to call the likes of us. As he detailed the changes he's seen over the last three decades, he surprised me by saying he salvages artifacts, such as furniture, fixtures and decorations, paperwork and other souvenirs, from dumpsters when refurbishing is underway. A lot changed, and disappeared forever, during an extensive renovation that took place between 1973 and 1976 in an effort to "warm it up a bit from the cold marble look." Although CP maintains a formal archive in Montreal, one that greatly impressed me during my visit, there is no procedure for retrieving and preserving parts of a hotel that is being remodelled or refurbished. Much of it simply disappears. From a roomful of original chairs from the Royal York's sumptuous Venetian Café, each exquisitely carved and fabulously decorated, upholstered in deep blue satin, only four remain. Staff and guests, of course, have always preserved a few bits and pieces in the privacy of their own homes — a "borrowed" place setting or napkin ring, an ashtray or wine glass, towels — and hotels occasionally hold an amnesty to recover such items, especially during anniversary celebrations.

We returned to the main lobby to admire the ceiling. Held by glue to the wood above it, a magnificent hand-painted canvas depicting historic heraldry and national motifs covers almost 12,000 square feet. In subdued colours, many set off by gold borders, I see the harp of Ireland, the Scottish thistle, and the flags and shields of the Houses of Lancaster and York, northern England adversaries during the fifteenth-century War of the Roses. A red rose for Lancashire, and a white one for my birthplace of Yorkshire.

It was cheaper to stay at the Royal York as a patient than book into the local hospital. Photo: The Royal York Hotel

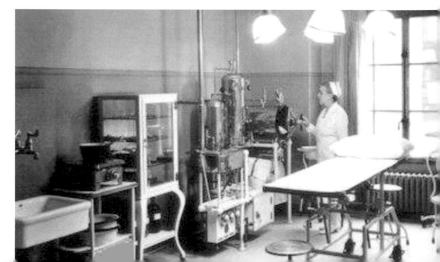

The Royal York was busier than usual for a September week-day morning and Tom left me to attend to more serious business. The NATO Security Council was meeting in the nearby Toronto Convention Centre and had filled the hotel with its twenty-four delegations representing nineteen countries. They brought along a few hundred police, military types in flak jackets and "undercover" security people who patrolled hallways and stuck out like sore thumbs as they stood around in cheap suits and new haircuts, resembling bored cousins at a wedding. As Tom said to me as he left, "Everyone's so busy looking serious that no one's really keeping an eye on any-one."

With my black briefcase and camera tripod in its long, black canvas bag, I made a fair stab, I thought, at looking like a terrorist, but I strolled around the hotel completely unchal-lenged. Well, almost. While viewing the themed meeting rooms, each decorated according to a Canadian province's industry and geography (Alberta's room has leather hides bearing brands from each of the pioneer ranches on the wall, British Columbia has a mural of tugboats pulling log booms — I'm sure you get the idea) I stumbled upon half a dozen of Toronto's finest eating lunch from a stack of white cardboard boxes. "Are you a terrorist?" said one, glancing my way.

"No," I said.

"Good, wanna sandwich?"

I did want one, but more than that I wanted to see the old private hospital, or what remained of it. I wondered if it would cope with the carnage that all the hired artillery might unleash if I took the wrong photo of the wrong UN person at the wrong time. At the back of the mezzanine level I found the hospital, much of its former antiseptic glory gone. NURSE ON CALL WAIT IF YOU WISH glared at me from a door, stencilled in white letters. Inside, on a small table, a blue three-ring binder held notes from staff that had signed out equipment, mostly wheelchairs and the odd walking cane or bathroom appliance. The small waiting room, with a couch and four nicely upholstered chairs, was very quiet, but during the

1930s the hotel had a healthy trade with the sick and infirm, so to speak. St. Michael's Hospital, a few blocks away, charged more for beds than the hotel, so many people would stay at the Royal York to be treated as outpatients.

I found the Health Club, fittingly, on the H floor and treated my cardiovascular system to a brisk walk through the men's change rooms, sauna, steam room, exercise room and poolside patio. All were vacant, with not even a plainclothes security officer in sight. From the edge of the still pool, cheerfully skylit from above, I looked out over a small green space between the hotel and the tall, black TD Centre. Feeling fitter and having worked up the keen appetite of an athlete, I made my way to the east wing lobby, pausing only to admire the brass Cutler mail system by the west end elevator lobby, and to stand for a moment beneath the four-faced brass clock. It has been a landmark within the hotel for generations and the words "Meet me under the clock" have been spoken by thousands. With no one to meet I suddenly felt quite alone and far from loved ones, but I also felt very hungry still.

Eating elsewhere in the city would have been sacrilegious — the hotel has a pantry full of culinary claims and records. For example, its kitchens are the largest in Canada and at 25,000 square feet could easily swallow the bodies of seven jumbo jet planes. At a pinch, if all public and private dining rooms were brought into simultaneous service, no fewer than 10,000 people could sit down for a meal under this roof. The Royal York also boasts the largest Ontario VQA wine list in the world and has a vineyard of its own in Niagara. For me, however, it was lunch time: tea would suffice.

I took a seat in York's Kitchen, one of ten food outlets in the building and a bright place, alive with primary colours and noted for its generous portions. A mural ran throughout the three sections of the restaurant, painted by local artist Leslie Abell in 1993, showing a group of animals buying food at the market, preparing it in the kitchen, then serving and eating it.

As I merrily chewed and crunched my way through a veg-

The Royal York's pool — blissfully peaceful, in spite of a NATO meeting. Photo: Dave Preston

gie burger and fries, watching office workers come and go, I wondered why nearly all so-called "family restaurants" look like a maiden aunt's living room, while here was a place kids would love but without a giggling one in sight.

Setting a good but totally ignored example to the diner on my left, I cleaned my plate. Serving up to six thousand meals a day, the hotel generates about 35,000 pounds of waste every week. About half of it is food, which is ground down and refrigerated until a farmer from High Hope Farm collects it to feed his six hundred pigs. The hotel pays him for doing this, as part of its effort to reduce environmental impact within the hotel. "Green Teams" of employees through the CP hotel chain strive to reduce water and energy consumption and compete annually for rewards that include exotic vacations.

I spent the afternoon talking on the phone to a couple of people who between them logged more than eighty-four years' employment at the Royal York. (And just as an aside: if there's one thing worse than being put on hold and being made to listen to awful music, it's being put on hold and made to listen to great music, so that when you're suddenly taken off hold you're in full voice halfway through "Born to be Wild.")

I spoke first to seventy-five-year-old Alice Cilcus from Saskatoon, who started as an elevator operator at the Royal York in 1941 when the war took away the young men that normally did the job. The operators worked eight-hour shifts with thirty minutes off for lunch; women took the daytime hours from 7:30 a.m. to 11:30 p.m. and boys came in for the night shift. Pay was twelve dollars a week and tips were rare. It was the elevator starter who had the real control — starting and stopping each elevator at specific floors, after being asked by the operator to do so. The starter worked at a large console and took floor number requests by phone from the operators. "The starter got to sit down so it was a better job," said Alice, adding that standing around for hours on end certainly took its toll on the women and gave her a back problem. Sympathy came to the rescue. "It was the CP president's wife, I think. She thought it was awful that we had to stand and made her husband provide us with chairs."

Appearance was everything. "We had to have certain hairdos," she said, "no big hair and we had to be very neat, in navy uniforms with white starched collars." Initially, strict rules of protocol removed the warm, human touch, making Alice and her colleagues little more than well-groomed robots. "We were told don't stare at people, don't talk to them at all and don't offer any greeting unless they speak first." The end of the war brought the dawn of Public Relations, and instructions for Alice to say "Good morning, sir" (or madam). Could

"Have a nice day now!" be far over the courtesy horizon? Taking Queen Elizabeth and Prince Philip to their floor during a visit, Alice had to refrain from having any conversation with her famous passengers. "I was told definitely not to speak to either of them or even to look at them, but he kept asking me questions, and you know, and, well, I just wasn't supposed to answer." Forty years later her voice still carries the frustration of the event. Being able to tell your grandchildren that you ignored Prince Philip probably doesn't have the same panache as relating a conversation you had with him.

Alice isn't sure when the elevators became automatic, allowing guests to select a floor by pressing a button, but she remembers one of the immediate side effects. "There were some very crude remarks carved on the elevator walls." Seeing the beautiful mahogany walls, I wondered how anyone could bring themselves and a penknife to do such a thing. Her career had its lighter moments, such as the time she opened the elevator door to see a kangaroo bounding towards her. She didn't give it a ride; it simply turned around and hopped back down the hallway to its room. She fondly remembers the cheeky bellboys, too, who would track down any servicemen that were entertaining lady friends in the rooms. The bellboy would knock loudly on the door and say the serviceman's wife was waiting downstairs in the lobby.

The hotel has certainly seen a lot of love in uniform. Among the thousands of men who were married on the eve of their departure to the Second World War, many spent a luxurious, unforgettable wedding night at the Royal York. The following morning, a painfully convenient train stood waiting across the street to take the groom off to the fight. Between 1994 and 1996, hotel staff thrilled at the sight of couples returning in their hundreds to inundate the place with fiftieth wedding anniversary celebrations.

Frank Daly is an easy man to talk to, and apart from opening more than a million car doors, talking is what he did for a living during a forty-year career. Fresh out of the army in 1945, he worked as a taxi starter at the Royal York, pressing a button to summon vehicles around from the east side to the hotel's front door. Though he wore a CP uniform, his official employer was the Deluxe Cab Company and he made twenty dollars a week plus a nickel for every cab he called. Within three years he became a doorman proper, greeting guests as they came and went and parking cars during his 11:00 p.m. to 7:00 a.m. shift. "I'd park seven hundred cars some nights, and it was fifteen years before I got Saturday and Sunday off," he said. He enjoyed his job immensely, in spite of the brutal Toronto weather. "Winters were tough," he told me. "And there were no buildings to the south then, so the wind and snow came straight in off the lake." Not allowed to stand indoors, Frank spent his nights on the front steps, speaking to anyone that came by, drunks and bums included. "I used to tell the drunks that we powered the elevators by turning the revolving doors," he laughed. No one ever gave him any real trouble, but he once chased down a robber fleeing from the hotel's Bank of Montreal office and sat on him until the police arrived. "I was so happy to see the cop show up I kissed his motorcyle!"

According to Frank, the sidewalk world of downtown Toronto has changed. "When you greet a stranger now they look at you strange, and today's doormen don't make the money we did. It's not just a job, you gotta love it. I miss it terribly." It's obvious he does, and he spoke with deep affection about his life and his colleagues at the Royal York. When he retired from the position in 1985, one of the gifts he received was a car door, because he'd opened so many. Years of breathing the carbon monoxide fumes that drifted his way from waiting vehicles took their toll, and Frank also suffers from arthritis, which he attributes to the cold nights. But he regrets not a single minute. "I never made a million bucks but I made a million friends." And he does that so easily.

I woke early the following morning, and not by some accident of bedside Japanese technology. Although I was a dozen days into my trans-Canadian journey I was about to get on a train that I couldn't help thinking was the real start of the crossing, a trip of more than 1,100 miles to Winnipeg.

Instead of taking the underground passageway, I left by the Royal York's main entrance and stood on the steps a while looking across a busy Front Street at Union Station, perhaps seventy yards away. Built to last longer than the British Empire, the structure is massive, its 750-foot length taking up a whole block of Front Street, from York to Bay streets. The centre block features twenty-two stone columns, each almost forty feet high and said to weigh more than seventy-five tons. These are turned from Bedford limestone that nicely complements the Indiana and Queenston limestone used for the rest of the exterior. In the early part of the twentieth century, when rail was king, stations were built as both monuments and the main portal to a city. Union Station, like others of the period, enjoys the grand Beaux-Arts style. It was designed by a team of architects from the Montreal firm of G.A. Ross and R.H. MacDonald, Hugh Jones of the CPR and John M. Lyle of Toronto. Tall Roman letters carved into the stone, high on the front of the station — "Union Station Erected by the Toronto Terminus Railway Company" — are flanked on either side by "Canadian Pacific Railway" and "Grand Trunk Railway."

Construction of this third Toronto Union Station began in 1913, but the First World War delayed its progress for several years. When Edward, Prince of Wales officially opened Union Station on August 6, 1927, he said: "You build railway stations like we build cathedrals." It opened for public service on August 11, but passengers had to walk across to the old station tracks. It wasn't until January 31, 1930, that trains used the new, elevated tracks. Union Station is a solid edifice, one of the few large stations on the continent to provide for through-train operation. Made to withstand the rumbling of a million trains and the pounding onslaught of a billion passengers, it's wearing pretty well. The building was designated a heritage site under the Heritage Railway Stations Protection Act in 1989.

The station is still run by the Toronto Terminus Railway Company, founded in July, 1906, and known today as the TTR — a wholly owned subsidary of Canadian National Railways and Canadian Pacific Limited. It's a terminal for rail commuter services and is a vital link in the Toronto subway system. Busy isn't a big enough word to describe the station's traffic; more than 24 million passengers using 55,000 passenger trains pass through here in the average year. There are four miles of platforms and more than 50 percent of VIA Rail's entire rail service rolls through here. Add to this the green, double-decked GO commuter trains, and the tally hits about two hundred trains every business day.

Inside, the great hall is spacious and lofty, with a magnificent ceiling arch of vitrified Gustavino tile reaching almost ninety feet high, and walls of Missouri stone, chosen by the architects for its light-reflecting qualities. Arched, four-storey windows flood more than 20,000 square feet of floor space with light, and below the cornice that surrounds the hall appear the names of Canadian cities and towns that the two railways served. Well-worn stairs at either end of the hall lead down to the arrivals area and the tunnel across to the Royal York that I had walked through about thirty-five hours ago.

I followed the signs down a sloping tiled hallway and checked in with a steward. After a dark walk along the platform, about halfway down a very long train with four dome cars, I loaded my luggage into double room A on car 121, Grant Manor (all the sleeping cars have similar, mansion-like names). As had become my habit, I walked up the track to take a look at the locomotives, three of them, Nos. 6449, 6454 and 6410. By now, thanks to a little homework, I knew these to be 3,000-horsepower F40PH-2Ds with a fuel capacity of 1500 gallons. Each engine is fifty-five feet long, weighs more than a quarter of a million pounds and needs a minimum turning circle of 140-foot radius, hence it slows down a lot for tight curves, of which there are plenty between Toronto and Winnipeg. Canadian National Railways put its first road diesel-electric passenger locomotive in service in 1929, a double unit weighing about 335 tons. Then, in December of 1937, Canadian Pacific took delivery of switching unit No. 7000, its first diesel-electric locomotive.

I met one of the engineers, Mike, who had been with VIA four years and drove only half the year, filling in for vacationing engineers. He invited me to join him in the cab after lunch, a few hours along the line at a place called Wasago. Happy as a schoolboy, I skipped back along the platform to my carriage and, since no one else seemed interested in doing it, shouted "All aboard!"

Toronto
~to~
Winnipeg

APRIL 25, 1955, WAS A HAPPY DAY FOR CANADIAN TRAIN lovers. Canadian Pacific launched its new, stainless steel, scenic-domed transcontinental passenger train *The Canadian*. This seemingly space-age, luxurious wonder would run between Montreal or Toronto and Vancouver. *The Canadian* left Toronto on Tuesdays, Thursdays and Saturdays and Vancouver on Fridays, Sundays and Tuesdays. The entire journey took just three days: you could leave Toronto at midday on Tuesday and arrive for a late breakfast in Vancouver on Friday. Hardly the supersonic Concord, but it was impressive, and the world fell in love with Canadian rail travel all over again.

But January 15, 1990, was a sad day for Canadian train lovers. VIA Rail slashed its passenger network in half and decided to run just one transcontinental train between Toronto and Vancouver. It would go via the CN route, through Winnipeg, Saskatoon, Edmonton and Jasper. The original CP line continued to carry freight but would no longer be used, in its entirety, for passengers. Rather than render a morbid chorus of Harry Nilsson's song, "Nobody Cares About the Railroads Any More," I'll give you a century-old pitch for the transcontinental service, taken from page thirteen of *The New Highway to the Orient Across the Mountains, Rivers and Prairies of Canada,* issued in July, 1900, by the Canadian Pacific Railway Company.

Next to the engine we find a long post office van in which a number of clerks are busy sorting letters and stowing away mail sacks. Then an express parcels van and then another laden with luggage. Following this are two or three bright and cheerful Colonist coaches with seats, which may be transformed into bunks at night and with all sorts of contrivances for the comfort of the hardy and good-looking immigrants who have already secured their places for the long journey into the prairies of the northwest or the valleys of British Columbia.

Next we find two or three handsomely fitted coaches for passengers making short trips along the line, and finally come the dining and sleeping cars, in which we are to live for some days and nights. The railway car-

Nine thousand horsepower all set for a long, diesel-thirsty haul to Winnipeg. Photo: Dave Preston

riages to which you are accustomed are dwarfed to meet Old World conditions but these in our train seem to be proportioned to the length and breadth of the land. The diner is elaborately appointed a marvel of comfort and convenience and we experience a new and delightful sensation in breakfasting and dining at our ease, and in luxury as we fly along through such interesting scenery. Our sleeping car is unlike the Pullmans you have seen in England, being much larger and far more luxurious with its soft and rich cushions, silken curtains, thick carpets, delicate carvings and beautiful decorations and with its numberless and ingenious appliances for convenience and comfort, it gives us a promise of a delightful journey.

My delightful journey to Winnipeg began at 10:58 a.m., as we left Union Station a couple of minutes early and rolled very slowly through a part of Toronto not renowned for its beauty. We passed under the looming needle of the CN Tower, a legacy of the empire built by CNR Telegraph that grew into a huge subsidiary company, CN Communications, that operates telecommunications businesses in several provinces. As well as being a major tourist attraction, the tower provides the Metro Toronto area with television, radio and mobile radio systems.

I climbed up into one of the dome cars and took the last available seat, next to a dark-haired, trimly mustached gentleman who introduced himself as David, a retired schoolteacher from St. Louis. Camera-happy tourists packed the car, but almost all were dismayed at the lack of colourful photo opportunities. The air soon filled with conversation, and within my earshot it included opinions on the crippling effects of union labour, employment levels and the stifling of free enterprise by socialist, lacklustre government. Not much of a holiday mood, you'll agree. I didn't say anything, but I quietly ached to remind my new (and mostly American) friends that their ride on this train was being hugely subsidized by that same lacklustre Canadian government, and that their welfare and safety was entirely in the hands of unionized labour.

Canadian unions, in a large part, were borne of the railway industry. Sadly, thousands of workers were savagely exploited during construction of the first trans-Canada railway and were too early to win protection against deadly working conditions, spontaneous lay-offs and racism. An estimated 15,000 Chinese labourers toiled on the CPR between 1880 and 1885, and the company saved approximately $3.5 million by paying them about a third of what it paid its European labourers. An extortionate head tax was introduced by government to dam the torrent of Asian immigrants who came seeking work — $50 in 1885, $100 in 1900, $500 by 1903 — but the rail companies either paid the tax or brought the workers in illegally.

Railway workers suffered for years during construction and were subjected to abysmal working conditions, impossible schedules, late payment, poor food and inadequate accommodation. Frequent dissension kept the RCMP busy and the police struggled to keep the peace during the 1882 construction period.

For more than a decade after the first trans-Canadian railway opened, those who maintained track and equipment, or worked on board the trains, struggled to gain respect and fair pay from their employers. Trackmen went on strike against the CPR in 1901, perhaps placing the final straw on the government's back, which soon gave way and recognized the importance and wisdom of labour relations. Two years later, the Railway Labour Disputes Act came into effect and several unions gradually formed and negotiated terms for their members with various railways. For years, railway porters were almost exclusively Afro-Canadians, many of them from the Maritimes. The Brotherhood of Sleeping Car Porters, an American union launched in 1925 to organize labour in the Pullman Company, eventually helped organize their Canadian counterparts.

Our train picked up speed as we went under a dozen or so

Daily hot hors d'oeuvres keep rail hunger at bay.
Photo: Dave Preston

maniacal lanes of Highway 401, but then we slowed to a stop and shunted backwards onto another track to change direction. Not long after, the first call for lunch came through the carriage so I heeded and found myself seated in the dining car, a cheerful but modest carriage that seats only twenty-four people. Half a dozen tables were picture-perfect, each with two linen cloths, pink over white, with heavy VIA cutlery (made in Japan) and white VIA crockery (made in the Philippines). I took a window seat, where a small white vase with real carnations brightened my setting, as did a pleasant couple from Oxford, England, sitting opposite, bound for relatives in Saskatoon. Lunch consisted of beef and barley soup, followed by a choice of main courses — quiche, focaccia club sandwich, Caesar salad or beef dip au jus. I chose the club, a single slice of focaccia bread with ham on top covered with melted cheese and asparagus, served with mashed potatoes. For train food, it was good. For airline food it would have been excellent.

Harold, the bar waiter, came around to welcome us aboard with complimentary glasses of sparkling white wine — my class of ticket qualified me for free food, but, apart from tea and coffee, I had to pay for all my drinks. Harold said it would make the journey and everyone's life much easier if we stuck to our sittings; that is, since we answered first call for lunch we should come to first call for dinner, at 5:00 p.m. Fine by me. (Breakfast runs from 6:30 a.m. for about three hours, on a first-come first-served basis. It would not surprise my mother to learn that I was never first-served.)

By 12:40 p.m. I was enjoying a cup of Earl Grey tea as we passed through muskeg, bright sunlight glinting off pools of open water and bleaching twigs and branches into skeletal remains. Tea finished, I tipped my server and walked back to my room to collect a camera and notebook before heading forward to meet Mike the engineer.

It took me five minutes to get as far as passengers are allowed, and when the train stopped at Wasago, just past a tiny building I took to be a station, I climbed down onto the track. After taking a couple of pictures I went around to the front of the engine. There was no platform so I stood between the rails, waiting. Eventually, Mike's buddy, Doug, hailed me up. They'd been a little upset by a couple of small but highly significant red lights that went on in the cab, lighting up what is normally a dull, grey panel when everything's okay. It was an electrical fault, and one that seemed to have them baffled. The three engines generate 3,000 horsepower each, but when they're also supplying electricity to the train they lose about six hundred horsepower. Engineers are strongly encouraged to save power, and fuel consumption, by being careful with the throttle and braking systems. That day, only one engine was supplying electricity, but because of the problem they switched to two. The cars are connected by 480-volt cables, which no engineer wants to touch while they're live, so any electrical problem means completely shutting down the power to disconnect or reconnect.

Doug had almost thirty years of service with the railway, coming to VIA from CN in 1992, but it seems that not many of the years were spent dealing with obscure electrical faults. Mike was at a bit of a loss, too. I made myself at home while they gently cursed the lights and discussed who to call and what to do. There are three steps leading down to a tiny washroom at the front of the cab, and a small storage space is tucked behind the door. A hidden black box in the nose of the engine records the train's operations and actions of the engineer — such as speed, whistle blowings and throttle settings. Everything but the voice communications over the radio is captured, but Doug thought even his chat would be taped for black posterity one day soon. "The days of making up lost time by going faster have gone," he said, "but these people are not too concerned, they're here for the ride." This is unlike the business folks, who ride the corridor trains and need to be somewhere very important very quickly. A clear plastic shield at the front helps keep bugs off the windshield, which should be as clean as possible at all times. There's a heater bar and a pair of windshield wipers, but freezing rain is the biggest problem engineers face in this climate. The cab also has bulletproof glass, "an essential for U.S. trains, especially in cities," according to Mike. In Canada, they rarely see vandalism or have anything thrown at the train. In fact, I noticed that people often waved at the train and the engineers certainly made a point of waving at anyone near the track. I suspect waving at railway engineers has roots buried deep in rural Canada. It's a wise practice, one that nurtures good will towards the train and the crew, and it probably helps deter vandalism of railway property.

The cab is cosy but comfortably large for two people. There are two adjustable seats with backrests, then a third one in the middle without a backrest. The driver's side, on the right, has a few levers and dials, and three communications radios: one to contact the dispatcher in Montreal or Toronto, then another to talk to the crew on board, and another radio similar to a CB, to broadcast locally to other rail workers and trains. There's also a cell phone that doesn't work very well or often out here in northern Ontario. Train communications have been evolving for well over a century. A telephone was first used to dispatch trains in August, 1877, at the Caledonia Mine at Glace Bay on the Sydney Mines Railway. One of the owners was Gardiner G. Hubbard, the father-in-law of

Alexander Graham Bell, inventor of the telephone and the man who installed two of them to control train movements.

Meanwhile, in spite of fibre optics, microwave towers and a following wind, Doug still couldn't get through to a colleague in Toronto on the cell phone, but he was patient. It comes with the territory. Engineers know their schedule six months in advance, working on a twenty-eight day cycle, fourteen days on and fourteen off, but not contiguously.

Back at the panel an idea came forth about flipping some switches, from VIA settings to Amtrak, as there was an Amtrak car tied to the end of the train. This was news to me, but apparently a Texas oil billionaire who loves trains had hired a private, vintage car, and was paying a rumoured four thousand dollars a day to be pulled around by VIA's train. He and his friend, and a chef, were self-sufficient in all other aspects, including electricity as they had their own generator. The penultimate car on the train, though, the VIA park car had no power, a major problem as twilight, supper time and a cold, north Ontario night were all on schedule to meet us. The switches were flipped, but it seemed to make no difference and the engineers decided to investigate further. A trek right down to the end of the train to inspect the linkage to the private car revealed electrical connections that were less than textbook. A large chunk of the four thousand dollars a day seemed to have been spent on string and duct tape.

We set off, red lights still aglow, and made good progress through the winding tracks of small-town Ontario. Fall colours were beginning to show, though we were too early for the real spectacle. Some of the maples were turning gold and brown, and the sumac trees glowed deep, smoldering red. I saw lots of farms with bright aluminum roofs and stacks of firewood, tiny hamlets and many road crossings, each of which received a mandatory whistling.

After smashing into a farmer's wagon loaded with fifty pounds of butter and eighty dozen eggs on May 4, 1833, George Stephenson thought a large whistle might be a good idea, to warn people of the train's approach. The whistle was designed as a musical chime — eighteen inches long and six inches across the bell, emitting a sound described by one early railroader as "...the squeal of a lawyer when the devil first got hold of him."

At every road crossing a white "W" sign appears on the right of the track. It stands for "whistle" and reminds the engineer to sound the horn. Unfortunately, real whistles went the way of all rail steam, long ago. Today, engineers press a large, square yellow button and a loud horn blares out the warning, but it's still called a whistle. There's a federally approved arrangement the engineer must play: two long blasts, then one short followed by one long blast as the train actually crosses the road. If the train's moving slowly the driver can extemporize, as musicians are wont to do when time's available. When the whistle sounds, a bell automatically kicks in and will continue to ring until the engineer turns it off by pressing another yellow button.

Ever since a dreadful September 15 in 1830, when the Rt. Hon. William Huskisson got run over and became the world's first railway fatality, we've tried to be careful with these hefty metal monsters. A 3,000-horsepower locomotive drinks almost five gallons of fuel an hour just idling, and when it's really into the sauce and moving at its top speed of ninety miles per hour, there's very little that can stop it in a hurry. Flesh is weak, and never more so than when it's pitted against thundering iron and steel.

Following a review of the federal Railway Safety Act in 1994, it was recommended that highway/railway grade crossing collisions and trespassing incidents be reduced by 50 percent over a ten-year period. Two more years of thought went by and then "Direction 2006" was born. This partnership between public and private sector railway stakeholders set out to increase awareness of the safety issues surrounding rights-of-way and grade crossings. For example, police officers are now told just how dangerous railway tracks can be and are encouraged to keep folks off them. Travelling by train is without doubt one of the safest forms of public transport,

but I'll perhaps aid safety efforts here by adding a few numbers.

Although trains hitting trespassers account for only 10 percent of total railway accidents, they rack up more than half the annual fatalities and a third of total injuries. During a four-year sampling period of Canadian railways, the most frequently reported train fatality was "snowmobile rider being struck by train" followed closely by someone "walking on the railway right-of-way." Only 11 percent died as a result of real accidents, while almost 40 percent died of what could best be described as "apparent suicide." Half of these were "lying on or between the tracks" when they were struck by the train. About a third of the fatalities died when they "walked, jumped or ran into the path of the train" and the remaining "apparent suicides" were "standing in front of the train" or "sitting on or between the rails," while a few were enjoying their final walk on the railway right-of-way. Most fatally injured trespassers were lying or sitting on or between the tracks at night. Hopping a freight isn't as easy as it used to be, either, as most reported injuries to trespassers occurred when they were "attempting to climb aboard a train and falling under it" or "attempting to pass or ride between cars and falling off." Of course, some were "attempting to crawl under a moving train." If ideas are a dime a dozen, dumb ideas around railway tracks are even cheaper. Believe me, there are safer places to walk, play or sleep off a hangover. Engineers don't blow the whistle for fun.

After being peppered with my questions for twenty minutes, Doug reached into his bag and pulled out a hefty Operations Manual, which seemed to contain everything you need to know about driving a train. I flicked through a few pages of signal patterns and soon got confused, then studied a page of track sections with the approved speeds for each one. The train must slow down to take certain curves, bridges or sections, and then speed up again. A passenger train must also give way to freight trains by pulling into sidings and waiting for them to pass. A lot of train driving, if not virtually all, is done by staring out of the window down the track, watching for signs and to ensure the track is not littered with large wildlife, such as moose and bear. (Or elephants. On September 15, 1885, Jumbo, the famous circus elephant, standing almost thirteen feet high and weighing more than seven tons, was struck and killed while walking along the tracks in St. Thomas, Ontario, by a GTR freight train.)

Basically, there isn't much automation when it comes to driving a train, apart from the steering, of course. The engineer is in full control of starting it and stopping it. *The Canadian* we were pulling to Winnipeg had twenty-two cars and I asked how long it would take the train to come to a complete stop, if we had to, from, say, forty miles per hour. Doug looked at Mike, who looked at me, then back at Doug. Brows were furrowed and teeth were sucked, and the answer, when it came, was variable to say the least. It depends mostly on track conditions — wet, dry, gradient up or down. Sometimes a longer train is easier to stop because you've got more wheels being braked. Transport Canada, in a wisdom borne of exacting scientific analysis and years of experience, says it can take trains "more than one minute" to stop.

There used to be a rail employee riding in the caboose at the back to keep an eye on things. But on November 14, 1989, CP Rail began running trains without a caboose, and CN followed suit just ten weeks later. So, when pulling into a siding, the engineer must estimate when he's got the whole train completely in. One way this can be done, according to Doug, is by counting telephone poles, which he says occur at a rate of forty per mile. This means there are 132 feet between poles, so ten poles take up around 1,300 feet. Each car is about 85 feet or so long, multiplied by the number you're pulling, and add 56 feet for each engine... still with me? I know I'd be pulling into the next station or reaching the Pacific before I figured it out, but Doug simply said: "You get used to it." As a backup, the other engineer on the train you're passing, or trying to pass, will broadcast over the radio

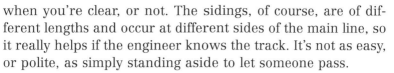

when you're clear, or not. The sidings, of course, are of different lengths and occur at different sides of the main line, so it really helps if the engineer knows the track. It's not as easy, or polite, as simply standing aside to let someone pass.

The manual also declares the approved speeds for trains on certain track sections, with freight trains always being a bit slower than passenger trains. Hence, if a passenger train is in front of a freight train on the same line it should, theoretically, keep ahead of it and perhaps gain a little. If it gets stuck behind one, it's stuck behind one.

An engineer should also know about any high loads or low bridges he'll have to deal with. For example, a certain U.S. train carrying three decks of brand new Ford sport-utility vehicles at a height of more than eighteen feet was not supposed to be on a certain section of track when it hit a viaduct measuring about sixteen feet, early one Monday morning in the 1990s. At least seventy-seven vehicles were knocked off the racks or otherwise damaged before the train stopped. A spokesman for the rail company said it would have been difficult for the engineer to hear that there was a problem, but he "probably would have felt a tug."

As light began to fade we pulled into a siding in Parry Sound and a technician climbed aboard and began working to get the little red lights to go off. I climbed down from the cab and followed Doug, who showed me how to get back up and into the train through the baggage car. Trains are far more lenient than aircraft when it comes to baggage, though allowances may vary from train to train. As usual for a civilized country, law prohibits explosive, combustible and inflammable materials, but canoes measuring up to eighteen feet are allowed, and there was a large green one sitting right there as I walked past.

A little after five o'clock I heard the first call for dinner, so I hurried along to the nearest dining car and sat with a quiet, smiling couple from Germany. Apart from the VIA staff, it seemed that I was one of the youngest people aboard. (I later met a young man from Germany and a Canadian born in the sixties, but we were certainly a minor demographic.)

After a pleasant cream of mushroom soup, I took the culinary tip offered by engineer Doug and had the Salmon Wellington, a delicious piece of Chinook in puff pastry with potatoes and vegetables, washed down with a very acceptable B.C. white wine. Dessert was a large, reddish piece of carrot cake, a similar colour to the scrubland going by outside. The setting sun prompted us and other diners to pull the window blinds halfway down on our side of the car.

A ride on *The Canadian* reminds us why the beaver is Canada's symbolic creature. I was to see evidence of the busy little bucko in every province. That evening, beaver lodges and dams lay strewn across myriad small lakes, and acres of drying bulrushes, swamp and birch stretched across the Canadian Shield to the horizon. Ontario is a bigger province than most of us realize, and pushing a railway across this forbidding land was indeed a major feat.

Coming up to INCO in Sudbury, hometown of Doug the engineer, the sun went down with a blaze of colour, lighting up the smoke from the towering stack and prompting a few photos of this remote, paradoxically beautiful industrial landscape.

At Capreol the train stopped to make a crew

A vintage American car hitches a ride at the back of VIA's Canadian, *for a hefty fare.* Photo: Dave Preston

change, so along with most other passengers I got off for a ten-minute leg-stretch and breath of fresh air. I said goodbye to Doug and Mike as they walked towards the station with their overnight bags. Capreol is obviously proud of its railway connection and had a small public display of a locomotive, car and caboose, and some signage. It's obviously not so proud of its vandalism, as the stuff's all enclosed in a compound surrounded by a high chain-link fence.

Underway again, I walked back towards my room and realized that as the light outside wanes and scenery fades off into the night, attention turns to the inside of the train. Things you've walked past a dozen times suddenly catch your eye. Enchanting stuff, such as a framed print, a phoenix-like *Bird of Spring,* by N.W.T. artist Aoudla Pudlat.

Outside my door I met Daniel, the VIA attendant responsible for my sleeping car. He'd been with VIA just two years, perfecting his sincere smile, and he enjoyed his work. "But it isn't a career," he said. "It's fun, we're like family and go out together when we're on a layover."

Poking my head into the cheerful but somewhat smoky bar car, I was beckoned into a seat to share a table with Jim and Jean, originally from Ayrshire, Scotland, but now on holiday from Heathrow. They're part of a railway tour group from the U.K. and were drinking neat brandy, at a rate that had the bartender scurrying to find more stock. When he couldn't, they switched to Drambuie, and offered me one. Declining politely, I nursed a plastic cup of soda water I'd brought from my cabin, but finally I accepted a vodka being poured into it. They were loving every minute of their trip, having spent three days at the Royal York before boarding the train. Their ambitious itinerary included Jasper and the Columbia Ice Fields, Kamloops, Vancouver and Victoria. And it seemed worth every penny of the several thousand dollars it cost them.

By 10:30 p.m. most folks were already in bed. A few staff were having coffee and a cheerful chat in the dining car, but apart from that the train rumbled as quietly as it could through the night.

I had promised myself I'd get up to see the sunrise, so I didn't really sleep, but kept leaning forward every half-hour to raise the blind, making sure I didn't miss daybreak. I was also cold so I remade the bed with another VIA "pure new wool" grey blanket and tried again to sleep. Then I got up, put more clothes on, got back in, checked the blind, looked for more blankets, remade the bed, used the washroom, remade the bed, and checked the blind. I finally decided to cancel my date with the sunrise and drifted off into a fitful slumber. Minutes later I was woken when the train stopped, only to realize the sun was coming up! So I leapt out of the blankets, pulled on the few clothes I wasn't already wearing, grabbed a camera and notepad and went up to the dome car, looking like something that small children fear lies hiding beneath their beds.

Six of us were gathered in the car at that point, watching the mist roll lazily over the muskeg and stretch out across scrubby woodland. A couple of late stars hung in a blue, lightening sky, but I couldn't see the moon. Even without the evidence of frost, it looked to have been a cold night. One or two passengers were joking about sleeping, or not. "The brochure said the train would rock you to sleep gently, I got whiplash!" Some did sleep well, and didn't hear the engine whistle, or the stops and starts, or the other passing trains. The black box of my body had recorded it all, however. Despite my aches and shivers, foul breath and ridiculous hair, I was pleased I made the effort to see the sunrise in all its morning glory. It lit up the leaves along the trackside, more yellow and golden than those of yesterday, with birch bark the brilliance of new snow.

A hot shower and shave later, replete with clean clothes and the correct body temperature, I felt I'd be accepted at the breakfast table. Grateful for my juice, hot oatmeal, eggs, pancakes, omelette and bagels, I headed back up to the dome car, where seating was already at a premium. I sat near the front and watched a hundred or more lakes float by my window,

A dusty pause at Sioux Lookout East for a game of give and take — the train picks up water and drops off garbage.
Photo: Dave Preston

some with small islands, most softly edged with downy fire-weed.

At 10:00 a.m. the service manager officially announced the time change, from Eastern to Central, though most of us had already changed our watches at breakfast. At noon we pulled into Sioux Lookout East. We were allowed to get off for "ten minutes" and most of us did, milling about the gravel lot and peering at the small, scruffy old station, a mock Tudor affair with very cracked black paint and cracked white stucco. As the crew removed garbage and the train took on water for the sleepers, I walked to the back and saw the rich old Texan leaning out of his private car, the Southern Intrepid. He was telling someone it was made in 1926 and had been in active service ever since, except for a three-year storage period after the original owner died in 1987. His chef, an old man with glistening skin the colour of melting baker's chocolate, leaned out of the back half-door, removed a fat cigar butt from his mouth and cracked me a wide, sparkling white grin.

The weather was sunny and warm and we were loathe to get back on board, but we were well behind time. We went straight in for lunch, first sitting, and I sat with a couple from Oxford and David, the St. Louis ex-teacher. Adriana, our dining room attendant, thanked us for being good passengers, told us this was our last meal with her and her colleagues, and asked us to please be nice to the next crew getting on. Because we were running so late, it was unclear if I'd get dinner on this train or not.

I wandered back along the train and paused at the kitchen door to have a peek inside. Originally, CP menus varied depending on the region being crossed — from St. Lawrence trout to Fraser River salmon. Local ingredients included Esquimalt oysters, Okanagan apples, British Columbia potatoes, Winnipeg goldeye, prairie grains, Quebec duck or Atlantic seafood...and live chickens, carried on the freight

---

A VIA chef works culinary magic in a few square feet of blistering-hot kitchen. If only airlines could do this for us.
Photo: Dave Preston

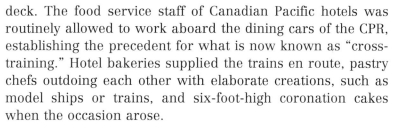

deck. The food service staff of Canadian Pacific hotels was routinely allowed to work aboard the dining cars of the CPR, establishing the precedent for what is now known as "cross-training." Hotel bakeries supplied the trains en route, pastry chefs outdoing each other with elaborate creations, such as model ships or trains, and six-foot-high coronation cakes when the occasion arose.

I spoke to Bill, the chef in my car and one of three on the train. There was also a cook who looked after the two coaches at the front. Bill had been with the railway twenty-six years and did a stint outside the kitchen but preferred this position, in spite of the heat. The kitchen is tiny, maybe sixty-five square feet and perhaps seven feet high, all stainless steel, and it's hot. Bill said it wasn't always that warm — sometimes it got damn hot, up to 109° Fahrenheit.

Bill had two hot plates and a broiler to operate, plus a steam oven, two freezers, a wall fridge with three doors, and three sinks. Even though some of the food is prepared off the train (such as the soup, which is made by a company to VIA's specifications, frozen in bags, then thawed and heated before serving), it's still amazing what a chef can do in such a space and under such a tight schedule. As soon as one meal was done, Bill was preparing the next. He fed seventy-two people three meals a day, plus coffee, tea and snacks, plus pre-dinner hot hors d'oeuvres.

Around five o'clock, the sun, which had burned its way across a clear blue sky for most of the day, was confronted by a bank of high grey stuff, somewhere above the Ontario–Manitoba border. The land was now much flatter, and as we crossed a small river the brush and woodland suddenly gave way to farmland, with arable fields, buildings, lanes and villages. Almost everyone in the car commented on how quickly the transformation took place. It was all very attractive, and I blessed the pioneers who took on the job of taming such prairie wilderness. When the CPR arrived here in 1883, a land-lease system let ranchers lease up to 100,000 acres for twenty-one years at the rate of twenty cents an acre.

Beyond a field of wheat stubble, two combine harvesters pushed clouds of dust across a distant plain, finishing off another year's harvest. Looming up on the left came the first trackside grain silo, a large, gleaming affair consisting of three circular bins and a huge tower with *Dugald* painted on the side.

Minutes later we saw the office towers of downtown Winnipeg emerging from the orange glow of a dusty sunset ahead of us. Winnipeg is about the middle of Canada, and I suddenly longed for the ocean that laps at a pebble beach just three hundred yards from my home, but I settled for a quick sniff of the Halifax Harbour water in the film canister I'd been carrying.

At 6:20 p.m. we slowed down as we approached the station, and I said a definite goodbye to my chance of a VIA supper. It had been more than thirty-two hours since I left Toronto, and I finally saw the turreted green roof of the Fort Garry Hotel, blissfully nearby. It would be my home for the next two days, and as much as I love music I looked forward to a bed that didn't rock and roll.

When William Van Horne first saw Winnipeg, on October 7, 1881, he was less than impressed, seeing its "streets full of garbage, egg shells, rinds of lemons and other forms of refuse cast out in broad daylight." (Perhaps he preferred stuff like that to be cast out in darkness.) Van Horne didn't comment on the number of drunks that the *Free Press* had written about: "They are to be met on almost every street corner at almost every hour." A few weeks earlier, the opening of the new Louisa Railway Bridge had seen a well-lubricated party. The city supplied champagne for all, including small boys who helped themselves enthusiastically, as only small boys can. When the booze was finally cut off, the ceremonial tent was torn down and the police almost had a riot on their hands.

From June of 1881 until the following April, Winnipeg

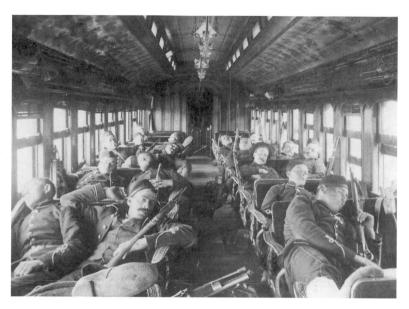

Winnipeg field battery escorting Louis Riel from Swift Current to Regina for his trial, May 22–23, 1885.
Photo: O.B. Buell, Glenbow Archives NA-3205-5

enjoyed a real estate boom, where fortunes were made and lost. (City lot prices didn't reach those levels again for another ninety years, in 1970.) Van Horne warned people not to speculate because of the new railway. The local community of Knox Presbyterians, however, put their trust in God and the avarice of their fellow men; they sold their church on a corner lot of Portage Avenue, which had cost them $26,000, for $126,000. The first tenant of the new development was the CPR, and, of course, a bank.

Winnipeg's population was less than two thousand in 1873, but by 1914 it had reached over two hundred times that, thanks in part to a bumper wheat crop in 1901. It was a financial, manufacturing and distribution centre for the Canadian West, but then someone dug a canal in Panama, fundamentally changing the trade routes and leaving Winnipeg to stumble down the dusty slope of the Depression.

Having wrestled my belongings off the train I took an escalator down and crossed through an underground walkway, then came back up to station level. I made my way through Union Station, pulling my luggage over the smooth concourse and through a doorway by the side of a central desk. I paused in the large circular entrance hall to photograph the impressive dome and stained glass windows. In 1913 the station was enlarged to include special waiting rooms for immigrants, and Winnipeg still has one of Canada's most ethnically diverse populations.

The station stands at the confluence of the Assiniboine and Red rivers, an area known as The Forks. Unlike many city stations, the platform is fairly open and raised, with a view down towards the river. Its green roof is a city landmark, and apart from that of the old Grand Trunk Railway hotel, the Fort Garry, it is one of few copper roofs in Winnipeg.

Stepping outside into the warm, bright, early evening sun, I saw busy Main Street still swallowing the tail-end of rush hour. The station has no neighbouring buildings and enjoys a pleasant, open aspect across the road to a boulevard and flower beds, bordered by elm trees that escaped (so I was told) Dutch elm disease.

We should turn for a moment to the other great railroad, the Grand Trunk Pacific Railway. The Grand Trunk had a 3,000-mile system with a main line from Winnipeg to Prince Rupert, B.C. Incorporated in 1903, it was built to compete with the CPR for the profitable traffic developing in western Canada. The federal government feared the Grand Trunk would ship its western traffic down its line to Portland, Maine, instead of to the Canadian ports of Saint John, New Brunswick, or Halifax, Nova Scotia. It was finally agreed that the government would build two lines, together known as the National Transcontinental Railway, between Moncton, New Brunswick, and Winnipeg, and from Winnipeg to the Pacific Ocean.

Construction began in 1905 and the Pacific line was completed on April 9, 1914, its route heading west from Winnipeg to Edmonton, then through the Rocky Mountains using Yellowhead Pass, and following the Fraser and Skeena rivers to Prince Rupert.

Steamships, plying the coastal waters from Prince Rupert to Vancouver, Victoria, Seattle and Alaska, encouraged passenger traffic for the Grand Trunk Pacific, but business never reached its potential. The railway went bankrupt during the First World War, with the federal government taking control in 1919. However, the company also built and operated the Fort Garry Hotel, which survived handsomely. Built by the Grand Trunk Pacific Development Corporation between 1911 and 1913, plans referred to the project as the Hotel Selkirk and the architects were our old buddies MacFarlane and Ross.

From my viewpoint at the station doorway, the Fort Garry Hotel stood smartly to attention, two blocks away. Two minutes later I was looking for a ramp at its entrance, up which to haul my luggage. There wasn't one, but a cheerful young doorman came to my aid and in the blink of a Friendly Manitoban eye, had me at the front desk, checking in.

Even though it was undergoing extensive renovations, the hotel oozed luxury. A huge and magnificent dried flower arrangement rose from the central table of the lobby, underneath a hefty gold chandelier. I noticed coats of arms in colourful relief set in all four walls over the archways of the two-storey lobby.

Heading to my third-floor room, I saw, beneath the brown stain of old carpet glue in the elevator lobby, an intricate mosaic tile border and marble flooring. Two broad swaths of wallpaper, one a faded grey and the other a busy blue, hung by three-inch screws, waiting, I supposed, for someone to make a choice (my vote went grey). The stairs were luscious, in white marble with heavy brass bannisters and gold-painted ironwork.

Room doors were mahogany with brass numbers, the same as at the Château Frontenac, but they were all painted, the outside a dark brown and inside, in my room at least, a pale blue. There was a transom, too, but it was screwed shut, top and bottom. Transoms used to be vital for air flow within hotels, for both heating and cooling, but they posed problems for security, fire and noise, and fell from grace. However, I was told that the Fort Garry was trying to figure out a way of restoring them, to somehow allow the flow of air but not the flow of noise.

My room, blue throughout, was on the east side, and I could see Union Station from my window. I could hear the rumble of traffic on Main Street and someone pounding away at hotel renovations.

Essentials unpacked and face washed, I grabbed an apple to munch and went off to explore. Following signs to a health club, I found myself on a walkway some thirty feet above the rear parking lot, en route to a neighbouring building. It was the Assiniboine Athletic Club, which hotel guests were welcome to use, and it offered a pool, two large weight and exercise rooms, a tanning salon and massage room. The facility is co-ed, though the only people I saw on my visit were tanned, gasping, thirty-something men pushing their deodorants to the limit.

That night, as I sipped my courtesy bottle of mineral water and prepared to roam around a luxurious king-sized bed, I wondered for a moment where *The Canadian* was right now, and who was being rocked to sleep — or not — in room 121 A.

Thursday morning came to me slowly, out of a deep and wonderful sleep. My window let in warm, fresh, prairie air, and I heard only one car horn during the whole of rush hour. Friendly Manitobans making their way, very politely, to work.

I skipped breakfast to enjoy the sunshine and wandered the Forks district behind the train station, which used to be freight yards and track but is now a popular shopping and sightseeing spot. Archaeologists tell us that people have been gathering here at the confluence of the Red and Assiniboine rivers for six thousand years. Fur traders arriving by canoe from the east were met by natives from the plains and northern tribes, with pelts to trade. Pelts have been replaced by fruit, vegetables and assorted trinkets, enough to pull in about 80,000 visitors a year.

Although these rivers have brought wealth to the city of Winnipeg, they've also brought perennial cargoes of hardship. The Red River valley has been subject to flooding for centuries, one of the first written records of this appearing in 1760. In 1852, Bishop David Anderson opened his account of a major flood with a quote from Isaiah (Chapter 18, verse 2): "Go, ye swift messengers, to a nation scattered and peeled, to a people terrible from their beginning hitherto; a nation meted out and trodden down, whose land the rivers have spoiled!"

But these tough prairie folk hung on tenaciously to their hard-won land and their way of life, in the face of repeated

Another Union Station, standing square and proud on Winnipeg's Main Street. Photo: Dave Preston

flooding — in 1950, when more than 100,000 residents had to be evacuated; in 1966; in 1979; and then the big one, in 1997. Towards the end of April that year, Winnipeg declared a state of emergency. More than 4 million sandbags were made to try and keep out the slow-moving, muddy waters, flowing through and around the city at a rate of around 138,000 cubic feet per second. Despite the Red River Floodway — an engineering feat that can handle up to 100,000 cubic feet of water per second, diverting it to flow around the city — thousands of people were evacuated and many had no homes to return to.

Steps led from the paved area of the Forks down to a walkway that runs along the river bank. I stared at painted blue lines on the surrounding walls, well above the walkway, that showed the floodwater levels from 1950 and 1997. I found them, quite simply, incredible.

I climbed a stairway up a tall glass tower next to the market building for a better view. I was overheated by the time I reached the top and then discovered that the outdoor viewing balcony was closed, as the roof of the building below was being spray-painted green by a work crew. The smell hung in the air like a thick veil. Retracing my steps, I came upon an Indian restaurant below, where I cooled off with an iced drink and ordered a crisp pastry concoction with delicious chutney. The makeshift breakfast was excellent.

I walked for miles along Winnipeg's broad streets and sidewalks. The buildings and pavements seemed dusty and very dry. The city endures a binary climate: bitter cold in winter and blistering hot in summer. People maintain a degree of comfort by staying indoors, but indoor Winnipeg stretches for miles by means of underground tunnels and concourses, and glassed-in walkways that connect buildings at the second- and third-floor levels. That day, in early fall, the weather was warm — approaching hot — so I descended into the cool, subterranean network, and within ten minutes I was completely lost. Hoping to regain my bearings I climbed stairs and rode escalators to try my navigational hand at the above-ground

Doukhobors arriving at the Canadian Pacific Railway station, Winnipeg, August 1899. Photo: Glenbow Achives NA-2660-1

system. I soon got lost again, but at least I had a view of the outside and I did stumble across a very nice collection of memorabilia from the *Winnipeg Free Press*.

Back at street level I soon found my way to the city's famous intersection, Portage and Main, and walked over to the site of the first CP hotel. Since 1970, the Lombard Hotel has been making a very simple architectural statement on this lot. The Lombard, named for the street it's on, is business-like in appearance and operation, and boasts more meeting space than any other hotel in the city, so I decided to arrange a lunch meeting with myself.

At a very comfortable setting in the Velvet Glove Lounge, I enjoyed a meal of goldeye, a freshwater fish available year-round from Lake Winnipeg, even when the ice is several feet thick. The dark red flesh reminded me of a kipper but it was much more tender and subtle in flavour. Surprisingly, it was completely bone-free. The citrus-chive butter, minted new potatoes and warm summer vegetables made it one sumptuous prairie luncheon. Hardly the ghost of a railway memory remains here, and I thought again of the Fort Garry's brass and marble and headed back there for a full tour.

Accompanied by Don, the chief engineer, I rode up to the hotel's seventh floor, a level operated by an independent company for about a decade as a casino. Safes, counters and other casino fixtures still littered the rooms as we explored, and plastic domes housing security cameras hung obtrusively from the ornate ceilings, vying with chandeliers for attention. It was a strange scene, ridiculous and sublime, heritage wrestling with anachronism. The casino gave the hotel logistical and reputational problems, but now the last chips had been cashed and the Fort Garry was planning to restore these two ballrooms, master-crafted in hardwoods and stained glass, to their pre-gambling former glory.

Downstairs, the elevator lobbies were being refinished in white Italian marble and the original mahogany doors replaced with oak. Don showed me the new corporate suite, a pleasing blend of old and ultra-modern, with hardwood floors and leather furniture, wrought-iron sconces, high-tech halogen spotlights, marble sinks, and a family-size soaker tub. Each room was devouring around $20,000 of refurbishing, at the rate of one floor per year.

Our conversation turned to nightlife, and I was encouraged that evening to go to the Convention Centre, just three blocks from the hotel, to witness the annual ten-day Oktoberfest. It didn't seem to matter that it was only mid-September, and though I was one of the first to arrive when the doors opened, the place soon got busy. I have more than a passing interest in beer, but the few on offer were poor, so I had a glass of wine and sat back to enjoy the entertainment. A yodelling

fraulein filled the air with song and an older gent in a tweedy jacket and funny socks became mildly operatic, then a large woman marched onto the stage to play cow bells, which left me helpless with laughter. Loud disco music took over and the dance floor heaved with Friendly Manitobans. There were groups of older women who danced to everything except the spoken announcements, middle-aged couples who glided around easily on the wheels of lifelong romance, and boisterous youngsters who barely passed the eighteen-years-old entry requirement. My late-night walk alone, back to the hotel, was a pleasant one, punctuated by giggles and the occasional cry of *Prosit!*

My Friday in Winnipeg was spent window shopping and playing hide-and-seek with myself in the underground walkways. I'd heard, during my stay, that the Exchange District was a good place to while away a leisurely moment or two, especially for those of us who like to punctuate the working week with a Friday Happy Hour, so I set off in that direction.

I soon found the district and asked a passerby for recommendations. A tall, thin man with a loping gait, he was obviously fond of the King's Head, an authentic British pub. He pointed me along King Street, so I wandered a bit farther, not overly enthused by the neighbourhood and its shabby, dusty corners and rundown buildings. I passed a parking garage covered in graffiti but only half-covered by a collapsing roof, and I was about to ask for further directions when I realized I was next door to the pub. I admired the heavy stonework and danced up a few steps to the door. Inside, the place smelled and looked like the real McCoy, packed with British bric-a-brac and every inch a welcoming pub. I looked around for a hale and hearty landlord and was approached by a red-haired woman who asked to see my membership card. Visibly surprised, I'm sure, I confessed that I didn't have one and I just wanted a quick drink. She told me I must either be a member or be meeting a member. The only other people in the room were two guys having a beer at a nearby table, who heard the conversation and noted my lack of credentials, but did not offer to meet me. Seems I'd found my first Unfriendly Manitobans. I was told I could join right there and then by simply handing over five dollars, but I declined and left the place thinking anti-colonial thoughts. On the sidewalk I looked back at the sign — King's Head Pub. The irony that *pub* is short for "Public House" was not lost on me, nor was the five dollars I didn't spend on joining. I walked back to the warm, windy corners of Portage and Main, then steered myself quite soberly homewards.

Ambling back to the hotel I called in at the station to see if my 6:00 p.m. train was on time, and it wasn't. A VIA employee told me, quite casually, that it was running about three, maybe four, hours late. She added that I might want to come

The lounge bar in the Fort Garry Hotel — who else could work here but a bartender named Angel? Photo: Dave Preston

back to the station at nine, even though she didn't expect to see the train much before ten. I was handed a slip of paper containing two handwritten phone numbers, so I could call occasionally to check on the train's progress. She had lots of these pieces of paper at the ready and it seemed to be something she was quite used to.

Despite its architectural loveliness, I wasn't inclined to spend more time than absolutely necessary at the station. Winnipeg, I know for a fact, is a fine city with a multitude of things to amuse and entertain the traveller, and a population of friendly people with whom to share the entertainment. But I'd been hoofing around hot sidewalks for hours, so I trudged back to the convenient Fort Garry. My plans to pass a few evening hours were hardly exotic, but they were scuppered when I arrived at the hotel to find that a conference had just ended and highly excitable delegates filled the entire lounge and bar. I found a quiet corner of the mezzanine where I sat trying to have a Happy Hour, sans drink and sans happy.

Later, when I managed to grab a vacant bar stool, I spoke to the bartender, Angel, who was young and blond had been working there for three years. She liked working for the hotel because it's privately owned, small and friendly, and "not like some huge corporation where you're just a number." She told me of the movie stars and famous musicians who stay at the hotel, but then suddenly panicked, thinking she shouldn't have because if it became widely known they'd stop coming. "It's like their home when they're here," she said. I promised to respect their privacy, changed the subject to food and ordered a Crusted Chicken Breast with French Fries, and a pint of Fort Garry Pale Ale. The evening started to look, and feel, a bit better. A little before ten o'clock I rounded up my luggage and herded it back to Union Station. I arrived in a fug of perspiration, and I didn't appreciate the warm night air, which is a shame, as it would be the last I'd get for quite a while.

Winnipeg

~*to*~

Edmonton

NOTHING BREAKS THE TIRED SPELL OF A LATE NIGHT WAITING room like the arrival of a big train. As excited passengers spilled into the station I gathered my gear and formed a polite line of one at the boarding gate. A VIA employee took most of my bags to my roomette, number 2 in car 123. The train, some thirty-odd cars long, filled the entire platform, the rear cars stretching back into the darkness of the Winnipeg suburbs. The delay, apparently, was due to the derailment of some potentially dangerous freight cars just outside Toronto, and passengers sat on the train, in the rain, for about five hours while someone cleaned up the toxic mess. My extra time in Winnipeg, spent at the Fort Garry hotel bar, hadn't been so bad after all.

We pulled away a little after eleven, but travelled barely a hundred yards before grumbling to a halt again. A train this size needs two service stops per station, to take on water and take off garbage. This would happen several times over the next seventeen hours as we squeezed a size-ten train into a series of size-five stations. We finally departed just before midnight and there was little movement along the train corridors, as both the dining car and bar service had closed for the evening. I wasn't sleepy, so I sat and looked out of the window, staring into the darkness, feeling like some guy in a Kenny Rogers song.

From here we headed slowly west, some fifty-five miles or

so to Portage la Prairie, following the route of the original CP line and the old *Canadian*, until it was replaced by the other trans-Canada passenger service, the *Super Continental*.

The Canadian Northern Railway incorporated in 1899, following the amalgamation of two small Manitoba branch lines used for hauling grain. Its principal promoters, William Mackenzie and Donald Mann, spent a couple of decades building it up to become a transcontinental railway with about ten thousand miles of track, connecting Montreal to Vancouver. "Canada's Second Transcontinental" was more a piecemeal assembly of small regional railway lines than a planned cross-country route.

By 1905 the line ran from Winnipeg to Edmonton, and three years later surveys were taken for a route through the Rocky Mountains. Yellowhead Pass was chosen, and the line followed the Fraser River down to the Pacific coast at Vancouver; it was completed by 1915.

There's more to engineering a train than a throttle and a brake, especially now the caboose has shunted off to that great rail yard in the sky. Photo: Dave Preston

Traditionally, railways were divided into management areas called subdivisions, running from east to west and south to north. Mile 0 marked the beginning of a subdivision, at the south or east terminal. Subdivisions were originally about 125 miles, the length of track that an average steam-powered freight train could run in twelve hours. Later sub-divisions were two or three times this length, which shows how much quicker we push things along with diesel fuel.

Along the route, the tracklayers made camp at various points and gave place names in alphabetical order. The CNR communities between Portage la Prairie and Edmonton (for-merly GTP) are generally still in alphabetical order — Bloom, Caye, Deer, Exira, Firdale, Gregg and so on, from east to west. Of course, settlements that pre-date the track spoil the chronology somewhat. Dunrea, Manitoba, is named for two early settlers, A. Dunlop and W. Rea; and two real estate men, Langdon and Ruth, gave birth to Langruth, Manitoba. Hemaruka, Alberta, is a compound of Helen, Margaret, Ruth and Kathleen, daughters of a former CNR vice-president, while a certain CPR station in Alberta was named by a mod-est group of folk not big on posterity: Seven Persons.

I slept fitfully that night, though I preferred the new arrange-ment in the double room sleeper, with feet and head in line with the direction of travel, as opposed to lying across it. When the bed is let down it fills the whole room, leaving just a few inches to stand on the floor by the door. Again I was impatient for dawn, pulling up the blind every couple of hours until I finally saw streaks of red across the sky, but I was too tired to get up and photograph it, so I stayed in bed for another hour or two.

At ten minutes past eight, I noticed we were about twenty miles outside Saskatoon, so I got up, showered, and headed for the second and last sitting of breakfast. I shared a table with a couple from Birmingham, who were heading to Jasper, Banff and Lake Louise, then going through the Rockies by coach to Vancouver and hopping over to Victoria for two days.

They were loving it, and I gave them a few shopping tips about buying maple syrup and native artwork.

Saskatoon Station is a small, isolated, blue brick affair, but it had the means to service our train, if somewhat slowly. By the time we pulled away, we were five and a half hours late, though no one seemed to care.

I strolled the length of the train, twice, and finally took a seat in the park car at the back. The scenery was unremarkable, flat and featureless, and my attention was drawn back indoors. American women around me discussed the public school system in Philadephia, and how effectively it was being ruined by minorities. The husband of one of these women had given an English woman a set of earplugs the previous night, which had bought her some sleep. (Talking to passengers over the course of the trip I found that some sleep like logs and babies, while others, including me, have trouble with the noise and motion of the train; it isn't bad, but compared to the solid comfort of a silent, stationary bed, it's enough to keep

The Canadian *gently winds its westward way around muskeg and swamp, blissfully free of highway fast-food malls and gas stations.* Photo: Dave Preston

sleep at bay.) Another English woman, travelling alone and barely containing her excitement, told me of her seven-week vacation. She was taking in Toronto, Edmonton and Vancouver, staying with friends at every stop. She's a living testament to the power of penpals and passports. Her husband had died four years previously and she led me to believe it was the best thing he ever did for her.

We talked about the weather, though no one had heard a forecast, so we looked at the sky and wondered. The Grand Trunk Railway often reported weather conditions to local farmers and communities along the line by displaying posters and banners outside the cars. Four types of weather flags might appear on the locomotive, each denoting a particular weather condition. As trains passed by stations, agents noted the flags and wrote up a weather report sheet to inform local passengers and station visitors.

The scenery became more rolling, the complete flatness of early Manitoba giving way to rough pastures, a few ponds and groves of birch and alder. Large Hereford cattle roamed at will and the odd combine dusted its way across a few uncut acres. The endless track spooled out behind us, mile after mile.

Apart from our schedule being ruined by the derailment, I noticed, too, that the six time-zone clocks in the park car were all to hell. It was 12:40 Eastern, 4:10 Central, 11:00 Mountain, and over on the west coast it was 2:55. I heard Sandford Fleming rotating in his grave. He's the man who, apart from working as a vital railroad engineer for the trans-Canada route, introduced standard time to the world. Until the railway began linking our country from sea to sea, every village town and city had its own little time zone, usually kept in check by a local jeweller or the town hall. It might have been noon in Toronto but 12:15 p.m. in Montreal, and perhaps 11:55 a.m. in Ottawa. Such discrepancies could wreak havoc with railway timetables, leading passengers to arrive too soon or too late for trains coming in from different time zones. Some of the larger stations installed several clocks,

Perhaps the crystal glasses and solid silver flatware have gone, but VIA's restaurant on rails stills pops the cork on fine service.
Photo: Dave Preston

each showing the various times of its region. As early as 1876, Sandford Fleming prepared a paper on his idea of one coordinated time for all, being adjusted along lines of longitude, about an hour every thousand miles or so. The CPR soon adopted a standard "railway time," so its employees would agree on who was late and who was early, but it wasn't until New Year's Day, 1885, that the Universal Time System was officially born at Greenwich, England.

At 10:15 a.m. we stopped at Biggar and a passenger related the tale of the famous road sign here that welcomes motorists. "New York is big, but this is Biggar." CN built a fancy rest facility in Biggar for its train crews. Costing more than $2 million, its thirty rooms provide a "home away from home" with soundproofing, blackout curtains, individual bathrooms, exercise equipment, heating and air conditioning.

I wouldn't have minded having a night there myself, but we pressed on, past bright white salt lakes and a lonely silo.

Crossing the prairies I found it was the weather that makes — or doesn't make — the scenery. The sky is the dominant feature, so if it's a clean, bare, pale blue, it doesn't hold your attention for long. The sun just hangs there, with everywhere to go, but it barely seems to move. Without stationary landmarks, such as tall trees or mountains, to gauge their speed, clouds appear to take forever to scud across this empty vastness. A rattling good thunderstorm would have improved the climate considerably, from a purely aesthetic point of view.

It occurred to me that an incident aboard the train might also brighten up the journey, as it did in 1932 along this stretch of line. On March 31 that year, Mrs. Driedger was riding a CNR train when she went into labour. The conductor, an enterprising Mr. R.W. Atchison, moved her from the coach seat to a sleeper, stopped the train at a nearby town to pick up a doctor, and a healthy baby boy was born at 5:30 a.m. He was later named Cameron Norman Robert, or CNR for short.

Up in the dome car I watched the flat prairie slide by, pockmarked by groundhog holes but with little else to study. We passed thousands of telegraph poles, set with millions of glass insulators, mile after mile of them. It was an endless procession, but someone cares about every one. Each pole was numbered, with silver-coloured digits carefully nailed into place at a certain height, running from one to ten, and then beginning again, with an occasional running total somewhere in the three thousand range. Someone else who cared was Boss Zoetman, who collected about 200,000 of these glass insulators and used them to build a model replica of his hometown, Pearce, Alberta. The world should have more such characters.

Outside, roving herds of beefy Hereford cattle grazed their way over unfenced miles of rough grassland. There were so many of them I wondered why we must destroy so much

South American rain forest to raise more hamburger meat... but it was lunch time and I, too, had to graze.

From the dining car I watched the land change from Saskatchewan to Alberta. It began to undulate, almost imperceptibly, then there were definite hills and small valleys. I saw my first nodding donkey oil pump, slowly dipping and raising its head. Then there were two more, then a group of three. We were in oil country.

Until quite recently, agriculture gave Alberta its bread and butter, and meat. Since the early 1960s, however, minerals have been the real moneymaker, and Alberta has some of the richest oil deposits in the world, as well as vast pools of natural gas. In the late 1950s, a few misguided scientific types thought they could extract oil by detonating nuclear bombs under the tar-bearing sands. Fortunately, their theory was never tested, but within forty years the province was producing over 80 percent of Canada's petroleum and about 85 percent of its natural gas. Alberta coal beds contain about half of Canada's known reserves.

An hour after my lunch of soup and vegetarian quiche, I broke the comfortable silence I'd shared with the people sitting opposite me in the park car by telling them we were at Viking. Seeing they were unimpressed, I added that Viking is home to Canada's only UFO landing pad, and their eyebrows rose high in unison. It was a trivial gem I picked up from a person I'd met at the Winnipeg Oktoberfest (though I forgot to ask why at the time).

Grinding stops to let freight trains get past us became more frequent, but finally we reversed into a spur beside a small brick station and arrived at Edmonton, almost seven hours behind schedule. Most folks got off to stretch their legs, and I got off to grab a yellow cab to the Hotel Macdonald.

Edmonton is an accomplished city, and one of its claims to fame is that on May 24, 1923, it was the site of the world record automobile jump. An open car with driver and passenger sped over a ramp and covered seventy-three feet before hitting the ground (and presumably destroying its suspension). The cab driver who collected me at the station reminded me of this daredevil feat. He was obviously trying to make up the seven hours I lost on the train schedule, but I clenched my hands, and a few other body parts, and tried to lose myself in local history.

In 1795, the North West Company established a post here, on the high north bank of the North Saskatchewan River, and called it Fort Augustus. The Hudson's Bay Company established another post nearby and called it Edmonton House, after an estate near London, England. When the two companies joined forces in 1821, the Hudson's Bay Company post survived, as did the name Fort Edmonton, and it became a major supply stage on the trans-Canada trading route. Initially, the Hudson's Bay Company declined to subdivide its

---

This is what two million dollars would get you, in 1915, but for just two dollars you could stay in one of the rooms.
Photo: Hotel Macdonald

reserve of three thousand acres, so the town of Edmonton set up shop away from the fort, and the cliff-top Jasper Avenue emerged as Edmonton's main street.

The Calgary and Edmonton Railway built its terminus on the south side of the River in 1891. Rivalry ensued between Edmonton and South Edmonton as both communities grew and prospered, thanks in part to the Klondike Gold Rush and the boom years prior to the First World War. South Edmonton incorporated as the town of Strathcona in 1899 and Edmonton was incorporated as a city in 1904; it became capital of the new province of Alberta a year later. In 1912, Strathcona and Edmonton were amalgamated, though the communities remain divided by politics, commerce, and a big river.

The yellow cab hurtled past the site of the old CN station, now a vacant downtown lot adjacent to the tall CN office building, and moments later we screeched into the forecourt of the Hotel MacDonald at the corner of Jasper and 100 Street. Seventeen hours of rail travel had not prepared me for such rapid starts, stops or sharp turns. I paid the driver and secretly bet myself he was from Montreal. I enquired, and I was right, and I promised to award myself a stiff drink as soon as possible.

It was towards the end of the local real estate boom, in 1912, that plans for the Hotel Macdonald were published.

A choice clifftop, waterfront property, complete with ambitious muskrats below.
Photo: Dave Preston

The Grand Trunk Pacific, using the architects Ross and MacFarlane, began construction in 1913. For two years, behind a large sign at the site entrance that read "The Macdonald – Chateau Type Fire Proof 250 Rooms," the steel girders sheathed with Indiana limestone rose. The building created a new skyline for Edmonton, at a height of more than 170 feet, and set a new architectural standard for the city.

The Macdonald opened on July 5, 1915, looking every inch the affluent railway hotel, but timing could have been better. Only the week before, fierce prairie storms had filled the valleys with water, and the North Saskatchewan River rose more than twenty-two feet to a record height, causing a city-wide electrical blackout and state of emergency. On top of that, the war had led to a collapse of immigration and tourism, so business for the first few years was scant. However, the Roaring Twenties brought prosperity and "The Mac" was *the* hotel for the area, right up until the 1950s.

In 1953 a tower addition was built, with far less taste and architectural flair than the original building. Then, during the heady flux of the 1960s, the ornate ceiling art of a grand ballroom was obliterated by purple and orange paint. What else could this herald but a slow decline? It culminated with the Macdonald closing its doors in May, 1983. A two-week liquidation sale the following October saw more than 15,000 bargain and souvenir hunters rush through the building. The addition, criticized and ridiculed from birth, was demolished in 1986. CN sold its hotel chain to CP in 1988 and finally, after a $28-million renovation, the Mac re-opened in 1991 amid waves of nostalgia and champagne.

I checked into room 732, noticing that the GTP emblem embossed on the door handle looked uncannily similar to the CP motif that appears on its original hotel room doors. The room was luxurious, with a long, southeasterly view down the North Saskatchewan River, winding its thick, brown way across the prairie. The king-sized bed was inviting, but I postponed my testing of it and returned to the lobby to explore.

I fondled the oak bannisters (as any wood lover would) as I stepped lightly down the marble stairs of the mezzanine. On the landing I passed a magician performing for a group of children and realized they were part of a wedding party. The bride, actually blushing, was being photographed below in the entrance hall, and along the corridor wafted the rich, warm smell of her extravagant wedding feast. My faded blue jeans were comfortable but hardly apropos, so I disappeared into the Confederation Lounge just off the lobby, where lacy curtains filtered the afternoon sun. A forceful acreage of oil painting hung over the stone fireplace, depicting the dour, whiskery fathers of confederation. It was comfortable but I was restless, so I found the health club and perused the massage menu — $55 per hour, $90 for ninety minutes, or $35 for a half-hour, available in your room for an extra $20, and appointments are encouraged. I didn't need encouragement, just a bigger budget, and so I moved on, past a mirror-walled exercise room and two squash courts, to the indoor pool and enormous hot tub, where I indulged myself for an hour, maybe more. That evening, after the stiff drink, I kept my date with the king-sized bed and showed my eagerness by arriving far too early, but my quivering anticipation was rewarded by ten hours of exquisite sleep.

I love hotel windows that open, and I always make use of them, but Sunday woke me with a harsh, cold breeze and a bleak sky to match, which made getting out of bed something to ponder carefully. I could hardly believe that a couple of days earlier I was too warm walking around Winnipeg in a T-shirt. Fall had fallen with a slap. I looked from my room window, now closed, across the river to several glass pyramids about a mile away. Curious, I asked a hotel employee what they were. Muttart Conservatory, I was told, full of tropical plants and so forth.

Tropical was a feeling I could certainly use so I set off, on foot, down McDougall Hill and across the bridge. A biting wind took chunks out of my face and neck, and I wondered

A view of the North Saskatchewan River from the Hotel Macdonald — on a clear day you can see the pyramids.
Photo: Dave Preston

what I'd do with the few dollars I was saving on a cab ride. Pay for post-frost-bite corrective surgery perhaps. Glancing down to the water at the far side of the muddy river I saw a muskrat, ambitiously building a dam out into the swirling current. Scurrying up the bank, it grabbed a small branch, then plunged back into the water with it, pushing and shoving it into place. I'm no civil engineer but I reckoned it might get another ten feet out before the river swept the whole twiggy enterprise downstream. Soldiering on, I found myself deep in automobile country, with nary a footpath or sidewalk in sight, so I leapt over a couple of steel crash barriers, ran across the highway and made a beeline for the glass pyramids, now within two minutes' jog. For a modest admission fee, I was allowed in from the cold and immediately filled my lungs with warm, moist, oxygen-rich air, knowing that I was really going to enjoy my time among the orchids and passionflowers, which glowed almost as rosy as my ears and nose.

The Muttarts, Gladys and Merrill, were Canadians who married in Edmonton and went on to make a fortune in local industry, starting with a lumber company in 1927. The conservatory was designed in the early 1970s and built with about $2 million from the Muttart Foundation, and help from the city and province. Thousands of visitors to this city flock to see Canada's largest shopping mall, but I'll spend my leisure time in the Muttart's pyramids, an ideal place to while away a few hours when Edmonton turns cool.

I spent the rest of my Sunday hiking around the cold, windy corners of the Strathcona district, setting a slow but determined course to the old railway station on 103 Street near Whyte Avenue.

The first CP station, a wooden affair, rose from this lot in 1891, and this new one opened on January 21, 1908, at a cost of $30,000. It's a classic railway era mix of French chateau and Scottish baronial design, one of only four of this type built in Alberta, all in the years 1905 to 1910. An old black and white photo by the door shows No. 4 grain elevator right across the tracks from the front of the station; the tracks are still there today, but protected by a new iron and red brick barrier. The last passenger train left here in 1985, but as I stood and watched, CN locos 3133 and 3101 pulled in with a long line of boxcars and freight. They paused and hissed for a few minutes, then, with a heavy rattling of linkages, began to reverse and eventually disappeared around a bend away to the south.

The station is now the Iron Horse Eatery and Watering Hole, with an exterior that's thoughtfully preserved. Inside, the industrial railway look has been maintained and the interior walls have been removed to create one long, cavernous room. Formidable boilerplates form the side of the bar; hefty, red wooden furniture and well-worn floorboards, exposed beams, ruddy paint and brickwork complete the scene. I admired the original sashwork on the windows and their sills of blond oak, in good condition. A few modern but tasteful waiting room benches stand around and if the music were turned off, I'd swear you'd hear the call of a stationmaster, or a whistle. The second floor originally provided storage space and accommodation for rail crews, who would be quite comfortable up there now in the cocktail bar with its plush leather couches, large-screen TV and immaculate washrooms. CP stations were built to last, and this one certainly has, with grace and style. I dallied long enough to sample a local beer, but took my appetite across town for dinner.

Two hotel employees, Karina and Karen, told me that the Mac has once again become "Edmonton's Place of Occasion." And this occasion, a 7:30 a.m. Monday morning breakfast meeting I couldn't believe I agreed to, was a rare one indeed. The renovation of the early 1980s was more of a restoration, and after our eggs, sausage and toast I was given a brief tour of the special rooms. On the eighth floor there's the two-level Royal Suite, which thoroughly impressed me, and if three thousand dollars had been added to my travel budget, it might have been spent enjoying a night in there. (A few days after my visit, Edmonton's golden son Wayne Gretzky stayed in the suite, his preferred place of occasion.)

Since I had arrived late in Winnipeg, and even later in Edmonton, I thought my trans-Canada train, scheduled to arrive at 9:20 a.m. might appear some time before noon, and I adopted a relaxed schedule. But as my little tour went by the front desk the concierge told me *The Canadian* was on time and was already at the station. Panic ensued, and instead of letting them guide me around the rest of the building I enlisted the staff to help me pack my bags and flee in a taxi. Of course, my racing-car driver from two days prior was not on shift — he sent instead his aging, very careful colleague, who had an unblemished driving record and would take all the time he needed to keep it that way.

Edmonton
~to~
Jasper

THE CREW OF *THE CANADIAN* WERE PROUD OF THE FACT THEY'D made up about two and a half hours between Winnipeg and Edmonton, and they were now going to enjoy a well-earned break. Lucky for me, as I'd arrived in the nick of time.

I checked all luggage except my camera bag through to my next stop, Jasper, then I went to the front of the train to chat with two men who were refuelling the three locomotives (Nos. 6444, 6448 and 6404, for those of you taking notes). The train had arrived with tanks just less than half-full, so each tank needed almost eight hundred gallons.

As usual, I wandered up to the cab and introduced myself to the engineers, Ed and Barry, who invited me into the cab for a chat. This pair had amassed seventy-three years of railway experience between them. Ed was sixty-four, all set to retire, and I could see in his thoughtful blue eyes that he'd miss it. They told me they drive the train out to Jasper and return to Edmonton, where they live, by taxi. It's a scheduled five and a quarter hours there by rail, and three and a half hours back by road, getting them home around eight in the evening, if things go well.

The first leg, to Edson, is fairly straight, they said, and the train usually makes good speed, up to seventy miles per hour, but then frequent curves slow the train down. According to Ed and Barry, we had about fifteen minutes until we were due to leave, so I sat in the cab and enjoyed their company until I heard the passenger crew on the radio saying all the doors were closed and we were ready to go. Ed and Barry didn't bat an eyelid, but I hastily arranged to meet them later for a ride up front and hurried down the steps to get on board.

I looked down the platform and it was deserted, except for one man who was now leaving to go back in the station, and he didn't work for VIA. For the second time that day, panic took over and I ran, literally, down the platform looking for any door that was open. When I saw there wasn't one for the entire length of the train I started banging on the nearest door. I tried to see through the windows and catch someone's attention, but reflecting sun made them opaque to me. Keenly aware of how foolish I looked, I knew I probably had the attention of about five hundred highly amused passengers but nothing happened, except that the locomotives throttled up and sent a roar echoing through the empty station. I frantically pounded on another door, wondering if there was a bus to Jasper, and found myself thinking: This is *exactly* the kind of thing my mother worries about, and with good reason. I

Another thirsty stop to suck up a few hundred gallons of fuel.
Photo: Dave Preston

promised myself never to tell her. The brakes hissed and I knew things were out of control and heading west without me, when a half-door opened and a VIA employee leaned out with a radio. I ran up to him with imploring arms outstretched and he said, quite casually, "Are you coming with us?" I gasped a feverish, "Yes please!" So he opened the door and I clawed my way aboard, with prickly armpits and a cold sweat beading my brow. Five minutes after taking my seat in the economy coach, my heart was still racing.

At 10:30, as the engineers prophesied (I now knew who was really in charge), we pulled out of the station and within minutes we were rumbling through an industrial area of cement works, lumber yards, scrap metal yards and a garbage dump full of seagulls. At Spruce Grove we passed a cemetery with lots of bright flowers on a fresh grave and three colourful balloons flying from a small headstone. My eyes watered.

We were making good speed, cutting smoothly through farmland and rough pastures. Raptors flew around or sat on fence posts, oblivious to the noise of the train. I noticed we were riding over concrete rail ties, the first I'd seen on the journey. Some of the line along here was laid twice. In 1916, the newly laid rails on the CN line from Edmonton to Yellowhead Pass were reclaimed to aid the war effort. Both the CN and the Grand Trunk were tracklaying and for many miles the two lines ran within sight of each other, an indulgence the country couldn't afford at a time of crisis. By the end of the First World War, some two hundred miles of track, laid at a cost of up to $28,000 per mile, had been ripped up and shipped back east, some of it all the way to France.

An hour later the farmland gave way to woodland, and fir started to appear among the deciduous trees. Lakes of every size had the telltale signs of beaver, some dams piled high and almost overgrown with vegetation. A crude, hand-painted sign appeared at Mile 116: Easy on Whistle Please. Ed and Barry know the rules, however, and we blasted our way safely over the road crossing.

At Edson we slowed down to run alongside a train of grey, bulk freight cars, each holding up to 5250 cubic feet of something or other. There were now more evergreens than yellowing deciduous trees, and the forest sprawled over the surrounding mountains to a heavy grey sky. We passed another long freight train carrying coal in open cars, probably heading for Roberts Bank, just south of Vancouver.

Western Canada's mines collectively have more than a billion tons of coal reserves, producing high-quality metallurgical coal used to make coke for the international steel industry. More than 14 million tons of cleaned coal are shipped annually, almost all of it by rail. Trains carrying coal to the Roberts Bank coal port, for export to Japan, are often made up of eleven locomotives pulling more than a hundred gondola cars, each filled with 150 tons of coal. That's one elongated pile of fossil fuel.

When we slowed down and pulled into Hinton, I gathered my camera and notebook and headed up to the engineer's cab. Hinton's page in railway history books is not a thoroughly pleasant one. On February 8, 1986, a freight train entered the main running line near here, instead of waiting in the passing loop. It ran head-on into a passenger train and claimed twenty-three lives.

Up in the cab, with Barry at the controls, we set off again and picked up speed. The engineers told me about the new braking system and its pros and cons. Theoretically, they could now stop the train well within a mile, though I don't think they expected me to feel comforted by this. When you round a blind corner in a car and meet something you didn't expect, there's often a place you can turn — onto a shoulder or grass verge. On a train you tend to stay right on course to meet whatever it is. Ed took his turn in the driver's seat, occasionally taking a brown paper towel from the bundle on the dashboard and wiping his armpits with it. He didn't seem particularly nervous, but it didn't seem all that warm in the cab, either.

We crossed the Athabasca River and Ed told me there was

a tunnel coming up ahead, one that sheep often used for shelter, so they sounded the horn well in advance. The sheep are fairly smart and don't get hit too often, though some are not sure which way to run when they see the lights. Railway staff has always kept an eye out for wildlife. The CNR took a boxcar out of commission in 1937 because a robin had built a nest on the coupling. A large protective sign stating DON'T DISTURB kept employees and the public at bay until the family had departed. Then, in 1943, a CPR freight conductor saved the life of a rabbit found in the path of his train. "Sandy" spurned an offer of freedom and rode back and forth with the rail crew, logging more than 100,000 miles in four years.

Ed and Barry regaled me with tales of odd passengers, including a man who wanted to travel with his parakeet in the baggage car; it was not allowed, so he stayed at the station

One of VIA's "Mountain Men" takes his train carefully towards the precarious curves and tunnels of the Canadian Rockies.
Photo: Dave Preston

with it and then took a two-hour taxi ride instead. Another man sat on the train and watched his baggage being unloaded at Biggar Station, even though he was continuing to Edmonton. In the baggage was his pet cat and as the train pulled away he broke down in tears, begging the crew to stop and go back. His wife intervened, slapped him, and negotiated road transportation for the luggage, and the cat.

Looking dead ahead through the windshield I saw we were leaving the foothills and approaching real mountains and Jasper National Park. Created in 1907, the park took its name from Jasper House, a North West Company trading post, which in turn got its name from Jasper Hawes, the trading clerk in charge of the post in 1817. Coal was discovered here, too, which in 1910 led to the settlement of a place called Pocahontas at the foot of the coalfields. We rolled by the town, what there is of it, soon after entering the park. Coal fed the hungry locomotives that steamed through the valleys, and the surrounding forest was plundered — or harvested, depending on your point of view — for timber to build rail beds and bridges. In 1930, the federal government wisely called a halt to the extraction of minerals and other resources from the country's national parks, so Jasper hung onto its remaining trees and coal.

As we approached Henry House we crossed a small bridge and I was told to watch out for a trackside grave. The engineers told me that Henry House was a civil engineer who helped build this section of track, in 1905 or so. (I later found out that the place was named long before the line was built for a man whose last name was Henry. As much as I enjoyed my ride with Ed and Barry, I realized that their history lessons and railway lore had to be taken with a pinch of salt.) As for the grave by the track, marked with a simple white cross and a body's length of piled white stones, I don't know who it is, but Ed slowed down the train and I paid my respects as we rolled by.

At three in the afternoon, bathed in brilliant sunshine, we slowed down and Barry jumped off to open a couple of

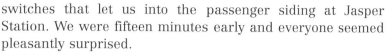

switches that let us into the passenger siding at Jasper Station. We were fifteen minutes early and everyone seemed pleasantly surprised.

I bid my engineers farewell and climbed down from the cab to wait with a couple of dozen others while our bags were unloaded. Jasper is typical of small town stations on this line. It stands around doing next to nothing for two or three days then suddenly a lengthy train pulls in and a torrent of noisy passengers floods onto the platform. Complete chaos is avoided by a polite but firm baggage crew. We were asked to stay behind a rope fence and take our bags from underneath it as they were pulled off carts and set down by the handlers. Inside, the single hall was busy, with folks trying to find their buses and connections, mingling with many others waiting to board the train.

I found the car-rental counter and spoke to Lydia, the clerk on duty. My car, it seems, was booked for the next day, but

Jasper Park Lodge, where Marilyn Monroe and a bearskin rug proved to be a dangerous combination. Photo: Jasper Park Lodge

Cute little bears still entice visitors to Jasper, even when they paw at hissing sprinklers on the golf course.

Photo: Jasper Park Lodge

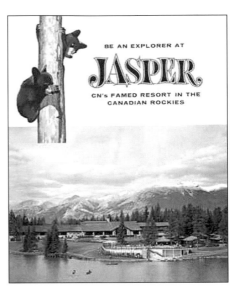

BE AN EXPLORER AT

JASPER.

CN's FAMED RESORT IN THE
CANADIAN ROCKIES

since I needed it to drive to Jasper Park Lodge, or JPL as it's known around there, Lydia used her small town charm and delicious smile to somehow make it work out. Moments later I was behind the wheel of a bronze-coloured Chevy Lumina parked right outside the front door of the station, studying a small map and wondering if her statement "You can't get lost in Jasper" was a temptation beyond my control. After a fruitless scan for local radio stations I stuffed some Van Morrison in the car's tape player and we set off along Connaught Drive in search of JPL.

It seemed only fair. The CPR was pampering rail travellers at Banff and Chateau Lake Louise, so its rivals, the Grand Trunk Pacific Railway, wanted a similar place inside a fabulous park to accommodate passengers. A letter was written by GTPR president Charles Melville Hayes on March 30, 1911, requesting permission to build "hotels and hotel buildings, buildings for employees, stables, enclosures necessary for stock, etc. and also the exclusive privileges of constructing and operating hotels and of supplying transportation facilities for passengers through and over roads and trails in the Jasper Park Government Reserve."

Exclusivity was not granted, but the government saw the

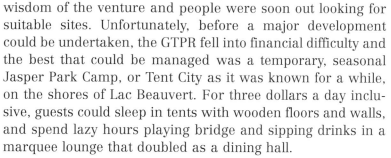
wisdom of the venture and people were soon out looking for suitable sites. Unfortunately, before a major development could be undertaken, the GTPR fell into financial difficulty and the best that could be managed was a temporary, seasonal Jasper Park Camp, or Tent City as it was known for a while, on the shores of Lac Beauvert. For three dollars a day inclusive, guests could sleep in tents with wooden floors and walls, and spend lazy hours playing bridge and sipping drinks in a marquee lounge that doubled as a dining hall.

In 1921, the newly formed CNR took over Tent City and added eight log bungalows; Jasper Park Lodge opened a year later. The resort grew, with design credit largely going to John Schofield, chief architect for the CNR system. During the winter of 1922 to 1923, "the world's largest single storey log building" was erected at a cost of $461,000 and formed the main part of the lodge. For sleeping accommodation, instead of a multi-storey hotel that would have seemed out of place in the setting, cabins were scattered around the grounds and waiters made deliveries of food and drink to each unit by bicycle. (They carried a tray in one hand and steered the bicy-

Open-topped cars carried visitors to Jasper Park Lodge from the station, so as not to miss a single scenic mile.
Photo: Jasper Park Lodge

cle with the other. One ambitious young man, convinced he could improve efficiency by carrying two trays at once, fell off his bike and was subsequently fired.)

The tourists came, in their thousands. The 1920s saw several expansions and the addition of a swimming pool, golf course and clubhouse. Business flourished up until the Second World War. Closed to visitors from the fall of 1942 until the spring of 1946, the lodge was requisitioned by the army during the winter of 1944 to house a Scottish regiment of mountain troops in training.

Tragedy struck on the night of July 15, 1952. Shortly after nine o'clock in the evening, fire was discovered in a cloakroom and the main lodge was soon engulfed. Guests escaped without injury, but Len Peters, a lodge employee, died from his burns after courageously escorting others to safety. At midnight the roof of the main building collapsed and it quickly burned to the ground. Thanks to the efforts of a huge volunteer workforce, and a light breeze that blew towards the lake, other buildings at the resort were saved. The Len Hopkins Band had been playing in the ballroom that night, and like the musicians of the *Titanic*, they helped maintain calm by continuing their performance as long as possible. The bass player, fearing for his wooden instrument, placed it in a boat and pushed it out into the lake. By seven the next morning, lodge staff had rallied and were serving a cafeteria-style breakfast of eggs, bacon and toast to 1,200 guests and firefighters. By June the following year, a new lodge building had appeared on the site.

On Saturday, July 25, 1953, about two thousand people, more than Jasper's entire population at the time, gathered at the station to welcome twenty-seven-year-old Marilyn Monroe, in town to shoot *River of No Return*. A special CN train took the actors and crew to locations on Devona Flats, about eighteen miles northeast of the lodge. Moviemaking began around here in 1927 with *The Country Beyond*, followed by such big-screen gems as *Under Suspicion*, *The Emperor Waltz* and *Rose Marie*.

Ms. Monroe stayed at JPL, but was not, as legend had it, kicked out with co-star Robert Mitchum for being unruly. However, she was turned away from the dining room for being "dressed inappropriately," having just come from a photo shoot featuring a bearskin rug. As well as her signature, the lodge guest book contains those of Sir Arthur Conan Doyle, Queen Elizabeth II, the Rockefellers, the Kennedys, Bing Crosby, John Travolta, Anthony Hopkins and Bill Gates.

CP bought the Jasper Park Lodge from CN in 1988 and carried out a five-year restoration project, and for the first time in the lodge's history guests were welcome year-round. More than 26,000 feet of meeting space and seventeen function rooms attract business clients from across the continent, come rain, shine or snow.

After crossing the Athabasca River just north of town and driving south again on Lodge Road, a wooden archway loomed up to greet me, neatly framing a snow-capped Mount Edith Cavell in the distance. About forty ornate black street lamps lined the driveway to my left as I continued into a thousand acres of resort. I parked outside the main lodge building and checked into a second-floor room in a peaceful block of four units right at the end of the development — peaceful until the geese struck up conversation. Hundreds, if not thousands, gather on the lake and golf course and almost every patch of grass to be seen.

My room had a lounge area, dressing area and bathroom, and a bedroom that could be screened off by sliding louvred doors. The king-sized bed had a plaid headboard to match the couch and armchair. There were two TVs and a handsome rock fireplace ready for a match, though a few hardworking baseboard heaters warmed the room.

Outside on my balcony, a few thousand feet above sea level, the air was definitely chilly, but I gazed for a few minutes at a northwesterly view that swept down to the lake perhaps seventy yards away. I set off to explore and take a photograph or two, wearing a shirt and fleece vest that I soon dis-

A rare moment of peace in the main lounge of Jasper Park Lodge. Photo: Dave Preston

covered was inadequate. The people I passed on the lakeside trail were tucked up in parkas and hiking jackets, but as long as I kept going at a brisk five miles per hour along the track I stayed warm.

I spotted a brave soul swimming in the outdoor pool, a-glitter with late afternoon sun, and then I caught a whiff of cigar smoke drifting back from the lakeshore where I saw four young people sitting around on Adirondack chairs, enjoying the lake view and a couple of Cubans. I wandered over and we were soon lost in conversation. They were American and highly impressed by the scenery, wildlife and value for money their U.S. dollar was affording them.

The golf course had a healthy crop of geese, and they were certainly not afraid of me as I wandered into their midst. I'm not a golfer, and yet I was enchanted by the tees, fairways and greens I saw before me, as are myriad golfers who come from around the world to swing and putt across these hallowed acres. It's a Stanley Thompson classic.

Born in Toronto in 1894, Stanley Thompson was one of five brothers who would dominate the Canadian golf scene like no other family. Stanley, a burly six-footer, played golf well, and he could design a course with a flair that few have shown since. Commissioned to create a course at JPL in 1924, his career was about to be driven into beyond.

He often spent three or four weeks walking through a property with just his can and a hatchet before taking pencil to paper. Here at the edge of Lac Beauvert he would capitalize on the mountains around him, aligning many of the fairways with a distant peak. It took fifty teams of horses and two hundred men to clear the site of timber and rocks, and the original bunkers were carefully patterned after the snow formations on the mountains. A million dollars later, the course opened on July 17, 1925, and Stanley Thompson, having built the most expensive golf course yet known, became an architect of international repute. Apart from the geese, other natural hazards make for an interesting round: elk graze on the fairways, ravens take off with golf balls and bears have been known to paw at the hissing sprinklers. Extensively restored in the 1990s, the 6,598-yard layout helped JPL scoop the "Best Golf Resort in Canada" *Score Magazine* award for 1998.

The afternoon dissolved and faded with the sunlight, and I saw happy players make their way to the Pike Lounge in the clubhouse. The temperature dropped another few degrees so I went back to my room, to banish the evening's chill with a hot bath and prepare myself for a dinner date.

I met Bob Sandford, the historian in residence for CP hotels, at the Edith Cavell dining room in the main lodge building. The restaurant is sumptuous, and I had to borrow a crisp sports jacket to meet the dress code, but we were soon made pliable by cocktails and passionate conversation about tourism and culture. The meal was exquisite — Fraser Valley quail followed by venison, complemented by a fine bottle of Chateau Neuf du Pape. Two hours later my head was awash with CP history and the lengthy cast of characters that helped weave it. Bob had to head back to Banff so I thanked the maître d' heartily and returned the borrowed jacket, wondering why Marilyn hadn't done the same thing instead of missing out on such a dining experience.

Wandering back through the lodge, I took in a few minutes of live music in the lobby bar, where a young guy sat playing a black guitar and singing a variety of songs old and new. People within earshot were appreciative, but the room was noisy and his music didn't make much impact beyond a couple of tables.

A happy guest, I walked back through cold night air to my room, cutting across the grass and glancing upwards, more and more often, to a fat moon and the star-studded velvet sky surrounding it, which eventually stopped me in my tracks. I was just picking out Orion's belt, or something of his, when I heard a loud snort in front of me. Lowering my gaze I met a large male elk, face to face. There was precious little space between us. Several options came gradually to mind, cloudy as it was after the cocktails and quail, and wine, and venison, and wine...and the option I finally chose was to rummage for my camera. I was still trying to focus in the darkness when the elk snorted again, loudly, and took a decisive step towards me. I countered with an auto-focus flashbulb shot, then turned and walked away. He didn't follow. I made it safely back to my room, still wondering if he'd caught the scent of one of his cousins on my breath.

I awoke to a dull grey sky and flat grey lake. It was still very cold and across the water I heard a chainsaw, briefly, and the lowly rumble of a freight train, I supposed, heading from Jasper into the mountains. People arrive in Jasper by various means these days. The train is still popular, but scores of tour buses make the five-hour-or-so drive from Calgary or

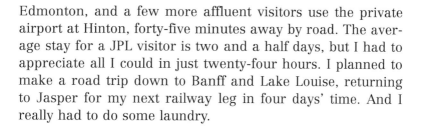

Edmonton, and a few more affluent visitors use the private airport at Hinton, forty-five minutes away by road. The average stay for a JPL visitor is two and a half days, but I had to appreciate all I could in just twenty-four hours. I planned to make a road trip down to Banff and Lake Louise, returning to Jasper for my next railway leg in four days' time. And I really had to do some laundry.

Jasper
∽*to*∽
Banff

THE MORNING WAS EVERY BIT AS LAZY AS MONDAY MORNINGS
should be. I slept in, took time to pack my belongings and add
a few Jasper Park Lodge toiletries to my growing collection of
souvenirs, then checked out. I explored the town of Jasper, by
car and on foot, and with all due respect to this fair place it
really doesn't take long. Certainly not a whole morning. But
after stocking up with film and snacks for the trip, it was noon
before I pointed the Chevy to the sign for Highway 93 and set
off.

Ten minutes later I was at the National Parks toll booth
and speaking to a woman who wanted $20 so I could drive on
through. I gave her the money and made polite conversation.
When I asked about the weather, she said, "Cloudy with
sunny periods, no snow until Thursday." I thanked her and
continued, the sky so grey and solid I wondered how it managed to hang above me, and the air bone-chilling cold. Jasper
National Park attracts almost 2 million people a year, and I
suspect they don't come for the tanning possibilities.

One of the main differences between travelling by train
and travelling by car is that in the latter you must remember
to steer. After days of blissfully watching the scenery roll by
through a railway carriage window, I'd become quite used to
the idea of not being in control of the vehicle. However, the
Jasper to Banff road is not a place to lose your concentration
at the wheel, unless you want to plummet into a deep valley,

Whether by steam locomotive or diesel, the best way to see the Rocky Mountains may always be by train.

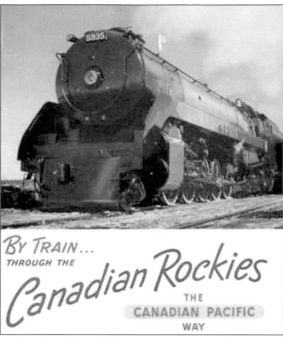

BY TRAIN...
THROUGH THE *Canadian Rockies*
THE
CANADIAN PACIFIC
WAY

stopping only when you reach the swirling frigid waters of the Athabasca River. Oddly enough, this icy torrent is home to the colourful harlequin duck, the only fowl on the continent brave or foolish enough to make its nest on whitewater rivers. The number of harlequin seriously declined in the 1980s, coinciding with the substantial increase of whitewater rafting trips operating in the park. Park officials, putting two and two together, now close certain areas during spring to let the ducks nest in peace. Or as much peace as a duck can get on a raging whitewater river during the spring runoff.

The scenery along this route is spectacular, though sometimes you arrive at a place knowing you're too late to get the best view. The magnificent mountains of Jasper National Park, as tall and grand as they are, used to be twice the size. Tourists of several hundred million years ago would have seen these peaks in all their post-upheaval glory. However, the road beneath my tires is but sixty years old, and it takes me along an incredible valley, with awesome peaks of about ten thousand feet rising all around.

About nine thousand years ago the first humans crossed this area, seeking the simple things in life — food, shelter, a place to hunt and quarry, friendly neighbours — and leaving behind simple stone tools. These people apparently came again, this time seeking fresh water when the prairies to the east suffered a severe drought, but apart from that, little is known of the first inhabitants of this region.

Along the road I saw a vehicle pulled over and I slowed down, prepared to lend a hand or give directions, which on this road means simply continue or turn back. Then I saw the driver, a short man in a brown jacket, outside the vehicle, pointing a camera across the road to the forest on the left. As I pulled onto the shoulder behind him I saw the object of his desire — a large female black bear and her cub. No one spoke, and he crossed the road to get a closer look and a better shot. I reached for my own camera and stayed close to my car door, which I kept open. I'm Canadian, and I know that black bears rarely attack. But the key word here is rarely. It's not the same word as never. And hell hath no fury like a black bear separated from her cub by a cheeky photographer, or anyone else for that matter. While he trained his lens on the wildlife, I trained mine on him, ready to record for posterity, and perhaps an insurance company, the first black bear attack of the season in these parts. I waited. He waited. The bears behaved and it didn't happen. The mother and cub continued to forage peacefully. Having spent all summer being gawked at by a hundred thousand tourists they were obviously used to it. He got his shot; I didn't get mine.

We were soon joined by a few more motorists, pausing for a bear snap. One woman climbed down from a southbound Winnebago and clicked away with a camera until the guy behind the wheel, anxious to complete the mandatory five hundred miles that all vacationing husbands must drive in a day, honked the horn impatiently. The bears leapt up and the cub scampered quickly up the nearest pine tree, sending cones and clawfuls of bark flying. Mama bear joined the rest of us in spirit by instantly hating the Winnebago driver, but she showed restraint by standing still. She stared back at us hard and sniffed the air, but decided she could tolerate the occasional idiot, as we all must. The gaggle of onlookers took a few last nervous shots then shuffled back to their vehicles.

I called in at Athabasca Falls to freeze for a moment, and then lost a bit more body heat on the gravel shoulder beneath Mount Kitchener. A few flakes of snow whipped by my face as I read a plaque at the roadside. Kitchener was first climbed in July, 1927, by A.J. Ostheimer and H. Fuhrer. I shivered and wondered why they did it, but then realized that July's weather must be so much nicer. As cold as I was on those fresh-air breaks, my goose bumps had seen nothing yet, and when I arrived at the Columbia icefield the landscape looked decidedly polar.

The icefield is massive, the largest south of the Arctic Circle, its glaciers melting into rivers that feed three separate oceans. The Athabasca Glacier here is the only one in Canada you can reach in the relative luxury of an automobile. Before stepping out into the fierce wind that rocked the car and sent ice crystals whipping across the frozen ground, I sold myself on the idea it was going to be worth it by reading again *The New Highway to the Orient Across the Mountains, Rivers and Prairies of Canada*, issued by CP Railway Co., July, 1900.

> The dense forests all about are filled with restless brooks which will irresistably attract the trout fisherman and the hunter of large game can have his choice of Bighorns, Mountain goats, grizzly and mountainbears. The main point of interest however is the great glacier. One may safely climb up its wrinkled surface or penetrate its water-worn caves. It is about five hundred feet thick at its forefoot and is said to exceed in area all the glaciers of Switzerland combined.

I pulled on most of the clothes at my disposal, grabbed my camera and got out. Wishing for gloves, I took off up the trail on a rough path of frozen rock and gravel. Incredibly cold as it is here, if you want to demonstrate the effects of global warming, this is where to bring your bundled-up school party. The glacier is losing more ice every year than it's making, so it's getting shorter. In 1890 the glacier almost reached the current roadway, where a large, stone lodge now sits with a parking lot full of vehicles, including buses with huge tractor wheels and tires for going across the ice.

Within two minutes my lungs were feeling pain from the cold, thin air. I wanted to get this over with, so I increased my pace, to get up there for a quick look and then get back into the warmth of the car. But I had trouble breathing. Before long my lungs were burning from an icy flame I knew to be blue. I reached the glacier and read a sign saying I should go no further unless I was an experienced mountaineer, or accompanied by one. I decided to make the Good Lord my guide, and since He built the damn mountains and glaciers I reckoned that was ample experience, and so we continued. It was bitter. The glacier was dirty and not the translucent, clear blue some of us think it should be. These days it's some four miles in length and about a thousand feet thick in places, but just fifty feet or so near the toe, which is where I was standing. The wind whipped ice pellets around me so fiercely I could barely keep my eyes open as I staggered around, trying to avoid the gaping cracks beneath my frozen feet. I came upon a young German tourist and asked him to take a picture of me with my camera. He had heavy gloves on and didn't take them off to press the shutter. I thanked him and scurried back down the slope, slipping and sliding to get back into the life-saving shelter of the rental car.

I suddenly realized I had a lot to do. For years I'd been saying it would be a cold day in hell before I did such and such. That day had come.

Twenty minutes later, and ten miles down the road, I still couldn't take a full breath without coughing, and singing along to the tape in the player was a cruel joke. By four in the afternoon my body temperature felt like it was back to normal, and I was passing Bow Lake. An hour later I pulled into Banff under a sky that threatened to drop a mountain of snow.

Fancy dining cars were all very well, with their extravagant cut glass, silverware and expensive crockery with exotic menus to match, but they posed a weighty problem to early railway engineers. Hauling such hefty opulence over the steep inclines of the Rocky Mountains was impossible in the 1880s, so a series of rest stops were devised at which passengers would alight to take refreshment and fresh air.

Three small eateries were installed along the original CP line — Mount Stephen House at Field, Glacier House near the summit of the Selkirks, and Fraser Canyon House at North Bend — where westbound passengers would have breakfast, lunch and dinner respectively. In the summer of 1886, dining cars were parked at the sites to serve the passengers. People were given time for a meal and a short walk before the train proceeded, but the spectacular scenery in all three locations had them smitten. Rail travellers were soon longing to spend a night or two in the rare mountain air.

The first hotels were quite small, little more than dining halls with half a dozen rooms for overnight guests, but expansions were unavoidable, particularly at Glacier House and Mount Stephen House, both of which became major facilities. Thomas Sorby designed the three hotels in consultation with William Van Horne, who took a keen interest in the project. Mount Stephen House opened in the fall of 1886 and the other two were ready a year later.

Even while these were being built, Van Horne was hatching a far grander scheme to capitalize on the beauty of the eastern Rockies, at the confluence of the Spray and Bow rivers. A village known simply as Siding 29 had been established by and for the CPR, but in 1885 it was renamed in honour of CPR's president George Stephen, after his native Banffshire in Scotland.

Enamoured of the architect's work on summer hotels and cottages in New England, his work in New York City, and the impressive parlour cars he'd come up with for the

Pennsylvania & Boston & Albany Railroad, Van Horne coaxed Bruce Price away from the U.S. to design the first Banff Springs Hotel. This was the man to preside over railway's marriage to tourism and, according to a newspaper report of the day, he was given "the entire resources of the Canadian Pacific Railway to draw upon, and hence it was possible to build with certain materials in certain ways." In other words, no expense was spared.

Those who have endured a household renovation know how difficult it is to keep an eye on progress and make sure the builder actually builds what we want. Imagine Van Horne's frustration when he made a long trip to Banff during the summer of 1886 only to find the hotel was being built back to front. The east wing was now a west wing, facing Sulphur Mountain just across the way. The fabulous views of Mount Rundle and the valley would be enjoyed by kitchen workers and those living in staff quarters, while high-paying guests would look at a tree-covered hillside. Van Horne's exact words were not captured, but he quickly made the

The middle-aged and the old — steam pulls alongside diesel at Banff in July 1952. Photo: J.S. David Wilkie Collection

builder a sketch of a rotunda pavilion, to be built out of the cliffside on stilts, so the guests could at least sit behind the hotel, which should have been the front, and enjoy the view.

Visitors alighting at the Banff Station around the turn of the nineteenth century might think they'd arrived in a bustling cosmopolitan city. Hacks and carriages lined up beside the station, their drivers calling out the names of the hotels that employed them. In premiere position on the platform was the Banff Springs "Tallyho" carriage, a large, stately affair pulled by four well-groomed horses. Up to sixteen lucky patrons could be taken stylishly up to the hotel in twenty minutes.

Banff Springs Hotel was immediately popular and immediately suffered growing pains. Applications for expansions flowed to CPR's head office and despite adding two hundred rooms in 1902, the hotel still turned away around five thousand would-be guests a year later. In 1910 the hotel sent about four hundred people back to the station to find shelter in railway sleeping cars at $1.50 a night.

Renovations were almost continuous from 1900 to 1928 in two major phases – from 1900 to 1910 on the original building, and then from 1910 to 1928 during construction of what became a new hotel.

Price died in 1903, so Walter S. Painter was commissioned to create the new Banff building in a blend of Scottish baronial and French chateau styles. Painter had been chief architect for the railway company since 1905 and knew something about the Banff structure. To refresh his mind on mountain resort styling, though, he undertook a tour of the Loire region of France, to gather inspiration from a few chateaux there. Before architectural students leap up and say "But there's barely a hint of the Loire chateaux to be found in the Banff Springs Hotel!" let me change the subject. But not until we agree that, yes, the arches are not lanced but circular, the dormers are not pointed but flat, the windows of the towers are not arched but rounded. It could have been designed by a wealthy Scot who'd brought back fond memories of France.

We should also remember that when the great French chateaux were going up in all their glory, the Scots were living in little more than big farmhouses. The first baronial castles of Scotland were fashioned after the chateaux, somewhat, and in keeping with Banff's name and appropriated heritage, perhaps Mr. Painter adapted his lines accordingly, and erased the effects of the English channel and a couple of centuries' tinkering. It's a copy of both styles but a faithful representation of neither. It might be considered unique, or if we're feeling patriotic, we could call it Canadian architecture. (And designed by an American working for a Dutchman using Chinese, British and Italian labour from a plan borne of Scottish and French themes incorporating Turkish and Russian baths...what better thing to call it?)

The eleven-storey tower, named after Walter Painter, took four hundred men and thirteen months to complete; a remarkable achievement for the time. However, the tower was built at a slight lean until corrective measures were taken at the five-and six-storey levels. Careful observers may still see a jog in the structure, if they have nothing better to do.

A second building glitch, discovered just prior to completion, involved the discovery of a secret dormered room that someone had forgotten to build a doorway into. It was fixed, courtesy of a crowbar and some colourful language, and all was well by the time the new tower opened for business in May, 1914.

In the early 1920s, the hotel was packing in more than 50,000 visitors a year, but at eleven o'clock on the morning of April 6, 1926, a fire broke out in the north wing of the hotel. By two in the afternoon a smoldering pile was all that was left, apart from some furniture that had been pulled to a safe distance. Two years later, the new southern wing emerged from a protective covering of planks and the indoor swimming pool had been fully enclosed. This meant that instead of the famous natural spring water, non-sulphurous water had to be used, to avoid gassing the hotel guests.

CPR president, Sir Edward Beatty, inspected the new hotel

Banff's "Castle in the Mountains" has no moat, just a raging Bow River. Photo: Dave Preston

when it opened in 1928 and was thoroughly impressed. Eight arched windows framing the "million dollar view" were glazed with enormous panes brought across the continent in a special boxcar. Unfortunately, when he walked through its $30,000 bronze doors to inspect the Alhambra Room he was less than thrilled with the oak flooring, just because he slipped on it. He immediately ordered the expensive, exquisitely crafted hardwood to be covered by carpet. That it was designed as a ballroom seemed irrelevant to him.

By 1930, the CPR had spent about $9 million on Banff

Springs, and along the whole chain of luxurious railway hotels, only the Château Frontenac in Quebec was worth more. Like most luxury hotels, a brief hiatus was forced by the Second World War but business picked up where it left off soon afterwards. When skiing became popular and affordable for the average Albertan, Banff finally realized the year-round potential talked about since the 1920s, and in 1969 it remained open throughout the winter.

Arriving at the hotel by car I circled the roundabout, with one eye on traffic and the other on a large statue of Van Horne in the centre, forming a sombre silhouette against the wintry sky. After pulling over and speaking to a hotel employee, I was directed around the back to the Manor section.

The Manor, linked by an attractive arched walkway to the main hotel building, used to provide staff accommodation until renovations created an additional 245 rooms for the 1988 Winter Olympics. While the rental car was being

---

A living room at Banff Springs Hotel — an electric fire but an authentic view from every window.   Photo: Dave Preston

whisked away by valet parking, I checked in. My baggage and I were taken to an eleventh-floor suite. As the Manor is built on a steep hillside, the elevator begins at fourteen and goes down, so I was basically at ground level.

The suite I stayed in had a spacious living room with a wooden fireplace surround and mantlepiece, built-in bookshelves and TV shelf, minibar and drawers. A glowing "fire" came to life when I flicked a switch on the wall. Maroon carpeting, beige wallpaper, a three-seater couch with two matching armchairs and two more upholstered chairs made it all very homey. A vase of flowers plus a bottle of sweet sherry and my mother would be ready to receive guests here. Down the hall I found a long thin bathroom with tub and separate shower stall, smoothly finished in grey tile and marble. The bedroom was small but comfy, about twelve feet square and filled by a king-sized bed. Like the living room, it had a view across the golf course and away up to Mount Rundle.

Poking around in the hall closet I found a small safe with a nifty electronic keypad. Whispering "We're not in crime-free St. Andrews any more, Toto," I made up a numeric password and played for a while, at turns locking up and releasing my watch, wallet, camera and Swiss army knife. If you change the password often enough and quickly, using random numbers, this game gets quite exciting, especially when you forget the last digit and realize you might never see your valuables again until housekeeping staff come to help you out. It's just the sort of thing you do when you're alone and bored, and surrounded by some of the world's finest scenery. After ten minutes of this I knew I simply had to get out.

It was freezing outside, getting dark, and I felt the overture of a cold playing in my head and chest, so I confined my exploration to indoors. In the Manor lobby I noticed an English grandfather clock marked "P.N. Banks Leicester" and a couple of massive buffalo heads thrusting out from above two gas fireplaces. One head was marked *CPR 1 — 1935* and the other, with equal affection, *CPR 2 — 1936*. Highland House, adjoining the Tudor House wing of the the Manor, has

The polished, mediaeval majesty of Banff's Mount Stephen Hall.
Photo: Dave Preston

a definite Scottish air to it. Lining the hallways are reproduction oil paintings of large, hairy Scottish settlers in a series of pursuits: getting off sailing ships, striding powerfully up the beach with pipes going full blast, ploughing land and helping tweedy women along rough tracks to a new homestead and a much better life...och aye!

I noticed a sign to the Henry VIII pub, followed it and embarked on a five-minute walk that took me outside, down a stairway and across to the golf course. I found the building, but after a cursory look around the place I turned back to the hotel. I found warmth and charm, and the "Castle in the Mountains" atmosphere that Banff became famous for, in Mount Stephen Hall. It was named for Lord Mount Stephen, first president of the CPR. The floor is of Bedford lime flagstones, and overhead great oak beams span the ceiling and feature the crests of nine Canadian provinces (every one but Newfoundland, which wasn't in the federal club at that point).

Stained-glass windows have the colourful crests and Latin mottoes of various CP officials. Edward Beatty's is *Modestia et Fidelitas* (modest and loyal); Van Horne's, *Nil Desperandum* (never despairing); and Lord Mount Stephen's, *Contra Audentior* (in opposition more daring).

A circular stairway leading off the foyer is made of fossiliferous Tyndall stone, with the grey outlines of creatures captured in a prehistoric moment, and the ceiling of the stairway is a marvellous example of "mushroom" plasterwork, growing upwards from the stone columns to curve smoothly and gracefully overhead. I roamed the halls and perused the gift shops in the basement concourse, then got a small bowl of chili from the cafeteria and went back back to my room for an early night and a quick laundry session in the marble bathroom.

The highlight of the following day was my trip to the hotel's raison d'être, the spa. The waters in the hotel used to be advertised along the lines of "hot sulphurous water gushing from the earth for the hypochondriacs to drink, and the halt, lame and withered to bathe in as well." Though preferably not at the same time. Soaking your body in this liquid elixir was said to be "especially efficacious for the cure of rheumatic, gouty and allied conditions...the liver, diabetes, Bright's disease and chronic dyspepsia." Since it was still freezing outside I thought I'd give it a go.

I was given a tour of the facility, then left alone, so I took a few photos. When I arrived back at the spa reception area, the manager told me I was not supposed to take photos of the hotel's private parts during open hours. Unfortunately, once you've taken photos you can't put them back. Two minutes and a sincere apology later, I was in the men's change room, a plush affair with red carpet and oak trim lockers. Dressed in swimming shorts, a white terry towel robe I found in the locker and a complimentary pair of plastic sandals, I was all set.

When the hotel first opened, a separate building housed a

large bathhouse, supplied with mineral waters piped eight hundred feet down from the sulphur hot springs on the mountain. Unreliable plumbing meant the flow occasionally became a trickle, but reliable hotel staff would secretly fill the pool with hot water and dump in bags of sulphur. Guests remained, as many a tour operator would wish them, blissfully ignorant. There were ten individual bathing rooms and a common plunge.

Twelve million dollars were recently spent upgrading the spa, and today you can have all sorts of things done to your body down here. It can be wrapped in seaweed or mud, steamed, soaked, or massaged and bound in warm sheets infused with therapeutic herbs. First off I tried the dry sauna. I was alone with the aromas of eucalyptus and menthol, a joy for the sinuses and I gave them ten minutes of it. Then I sat in the much hotter inner sanctum of the dry sauna, and toughed it out for five minutes. Next, I crossed the tiled apron of the indoor men's whirlpool, where two naked men sat talking about mountain bike trails, and entered the steam room. Again I was alone and it was hot and very foggy. I wouldn't have been able to identify a face at fifteen feet and I certainly wouldn't drive in such conditions. I managed five minutes then took a cool shower before entering the hallowed hall of the spa.

The hall is covered by a glass dome, but on that night all I saw up there was a glimmering reflection of the water, and I heard semi-classical, New Age music (without the whales) flowing from unseen speakers. The central pool has thirteen different minerals from the Sarvar Springs in Hungary, including lithium, which is renowned for stress relief, plus sodium and potassium. There are three small waterfalls in the glass domed pool area, each one a different temperature.

Three young women were already in the pool and they seemed to be enjoying it, floating around and smiling beatifically. I joined them and bobbed about, trying to taste or smell the minerals I'd heard so much about, but they were barely perceptible. As I put my head beneath the surface I heard thin music that was different to that playing elsewhere in the room. I recognized it as an instrumental, Muzak-type version of "Every Breath You Take." It was an improvement over the other stuff, with or without whales. The next underwater tune seemed to be without melody, though I held my breath and listened intently, and I realized that the other three bathers were also trying to figure it out. One of them suddenly leapt up and yelled "It's 'Lady in Red,' listen," and she sang us a chorus. I laughed and we continued this semi-submerged game of Name That Tune for a few more tracks.

I tried the Cascade waterfall next, its water a pleasant body-temperature and I imagined it might be like standing naked in a tropical rainstorm. Standing beneath a rushing waterfall can look pretty stupid, but it can feel wonderful. I splashed back into the main pool, just long enough to identify "Imagine" by John Lennon, then I walked boldly into the Assiniboine waterfall. Gross error. It was by far the coldest of

An illicit picture of the Solace Mineral Pool in the famous spa. (The author apologizes for breaking a hotel rule.) Photo: Dave Preston

The outdoor swimming pool at the Cave and Basin Hot Springs,
Banff is now just a dry memory of its former self.
Photo: Dave Preston

the lot and I should have prepared for it by running out of
time or something. I felt my body contract and my pores slap
shut. *Invigorating* sprang to mind, and a couple of other
words. Finally, I drifted over to the outdoor whirlpool, where
I warmed up and gazed up, looking for a star bright enough
to penetrate the night's thin cloud. I found one, then another,
and the evening was complete, my weightless body having
absorbed all it could take.

Towelled off and glowing, I browsed the spa's boutique
and thought about buying a pack of the magical salts to make
my own Hungarian *kur* bath at home. There were various
mixes to be had, with extracts of a seaweed, herbs, sea salt
and a range of minerals, but I declined, knowing the sensual

experience I'd just had could not be simply bought and dropped into a humble domestic bathtub. I passed the spa restaurant, telling myself I was slim and not hungry, and headed back to my suite. I felt good. Damn good. Beautifully indulged, refreshed, rejuvenated, highly energized and full of something or other. I felt I could do wonderful things that night. I could conquer the world! I poured myself a glass of cool Chardonnay to celebrate this sparkling new joie de vivre. And before the glass was empty I fell asleep on the couch.

The next day I took a drive through the village, turning right after the bridge, past some fine old riverside homes. The road climbed and I found myself high above the river, with a nice view back to the hotel across the whitewater of Bow River falls, the spot where Lassie became the first movie star to shoot these rapids, in *Lassie Come Home*. (What is it girl? What are you trying to tell me? You have hypothermia?)

I continued up the slope of Tunnel Mountain, so called because in 1882 CPR surveyors had a plan to blast a 300-yard tunnel through it. Then a surveyor named Shaw came up with a better and cheaper idea: to send the tracks along the Cascade trench, the route of today's Trans-Canada Highway. So there is no tunnel in Tunnel Mountain.

Down in the village again I picked up some supplies and visited the railway station. The building was attractively made of river rock and wood, but inside it was nondescript, modern and simply functional. Apart from a few track workers laying new ties with a big machine, the place seemed deserted. I noticed a large rail snowplough in a siding, and wondered how long before it would be in use. The sky was woolly and dark, and the cold surrounded me like a pack of hungry wolves, biting with sharp teeth.

On the way back to the hotel I made a detour down to the river and came upon a small group of tourists mesmerized by a grazing bull elk. Banff was having its "fall rut," when bulls scope out their females and can be quite aggressive. Female elk realized a while ago that Banff is free of predators and so the chance of raising their young is better, hence they hang out here by the dozen. Elk look benign and tourists don't appreciate the potential danger, so park wardens patrol the village early in the morning and try to drive away herds if they're too close to people, often using a yellow plastic bag on the end of a hockey stick. If the warden can drive the cows away, the bull will follow. Back at the riverside stand-off, cameras were poised when a local shouted to the group that elk often charge without warning. The bull started to move forward. A woman scurried back with her camera and took refuge beside my car, which I slipped into gear and drove away, leaving her with a fabulous if somewhat risky composition of an advancing bull elk.

My final stop was the place that gave this town its name. The springs. The first hot springs developed at Banff, now run by the federal government as the Cave and Basin National Historic Site, attract over 160,000 people a year, and I was the last to arrive that day.

Native people used these springs long before the arrival of Europeans; the Blackfoot name for Banff townsite is *nato-oh-sis-koom*, meaning "holy springs." Europeans first learned of the springs in 1859, but they were later "discovered" by a construction crew from the CPR in 1883. One of the workmen, Frank McCabe, applied for title to the springs and much legal wrangling ensued. The government wasn't keen on privatization, so in November, 1885, Ottawa set aside Banff Springs and the first 6,400 acres of surrounding land as a park reserve, "for the education and enjoyment of the nation." Following legal surveys and payments to those claiming rights, the country's first national park was created. It was known as Rocky Mountains Park until 1930, when it was enlarged and renamed Banff National Park.

A thirty-foot tunnel leads from the lobby of the building to the cave, which is roughly circular, about thirty-six feet across and eighteen feet high. Daylight filters through a hole in the ceiling, the only means of access until the tunnel was blasted through in 1887, but soft lighting shows the contours of the cavern and a rock wall contains the gently bubbling pool of mineral water.

The water is rich in sulphate, calcium, bicarbonate and magnesium, and a sour, sulphurous smell fills the air. Stalactites, formed over the years by the minerals, once hung from the ceiling, but they were broken off long ago by souvenir hunters.

Outside there's another mineral pool, home to a rare species of water snail. The original bathing pool, the largest in Canada when built in 1914, closed about eighty years later, and it's now a dry, Japanese-style garden bed of slate and rocks.

On Thursday morning I awoke to see the heavens having a silent pillow fight. Large snowflakes were turning the world white. The kettle made a welcome noise and after a second cup of Earl Grey and a moist bran muffin I was ready, almost, to tackle the drive to Lake Louise.

I asked at the front desk about the weather and road conditions and I received a warm smile. Not to worry, she said, everything, including the road, was fine, and the snow would limit itself to a few impotent flurries. I tried to get my money's worth from the valet parking and waited by the lobby's gas fire while the driver brought the car around, then I let it sit for a few minutes to warm up. I had no gloves, scarf, shovel, chains or snow brush. I was not ready for a mountainous winter. Not by a long, cold way.

Banff
to
Lake Louise
to
Jasper

THERE ARE TWO WAYS TO GET FROM BANFF TO LAKE LOUISE BY road: the fast, spacious, four-lane Trans-Canada Highway, or the winding, more scenic Bow Valley Parkway. I came in on the highway and was in no particular hurry to get to the next hotel, so I took the latter route, with a nervous eye on the weather. The speed limit for the road wasn't very high, but for once I stuck to it. More or less.

About an hour into the trip, thoroughly enjoying the wintry beauty of it all, I pulled over to look at the Hillsdale Slide. A major rumble some eight thousand years ago sent a good chunk of mountain rattling down into the valley bottom, making the landscape very uneven and forcing the road to twist and turn around the piles of debris, now covered by forest, grass, and a light powdering of snow. It makes for an interesting drive, and the parkway is especially popular with motorcyclists in summer, though not, I suspect, at the posted speed limit.

Although I looked and peered intently, I didn't actually see any wildlife, but the woods seemed to pulsate with potential. The snow, as promised, turned out to be but a fleeting taste of winter and the road surface soon became wet and bare. I hardly saw any other traffic, and I slowed down or stopped off a few times to look at the railway as it curved around the Bow River below.

The Castle Mountain Internment Camp monument caught my eye and begged a quiet pause for thought. Thousands of immigrants from the Austro-Hungarian Empire, some of whom were Canadian citizens, were interned during the First World War, from 1914 to 1920. At the roadside by the edge of the pine forest is a life-sized statue of a Ukrainian farmer, by John Boxtel. It is dedicated to those kept at the internment camps from July 14, 1915, to July 15, 1917. The internees became "forced-labourers" and were used to develop Banff National Park, among other things. They worked six days a week for twenty-five cents a day, pushing the Banff roadway through to Lake Louise to capitalize on potential tourism. And for that we should mix our shame with gratitude.

Though quick to label them "enemy aliens" under the 1914 War Measures Act, Canada owes much to Ukrainians. In 1842, an Ontario farmer named David Fife obtained a sample of Ukrainian spring wheat from a Danzig ship unloading at Glasgow in Scotland. He found it matured ten days earlier than other types of wheat, making it ideal for the short

Lake Louise Station looking its wintry best, February 1, 1983.
Photo: J. S. David Wilkie Collection

Canadian growing season. Although wheat had been grown in Canada since 1644, this new strain changed the country's economy. By 1928, nearly all of Canada's spring wheat crop was Marquis, a hybrid using the hardy Ukrainian wheat.

Immigration to Canada was curtailed during and after the war, as Ukrainians were considered "non-preferred immigrants" according to Canada's immigration policy. However, both the CNR and the CPR were expanding rapidly, increasing the demand for labour, so they pressured the government for permission to recruit immigrants from eastern Europe. For a while in the late 1920s, Ukrainian immigrants were again numerous and welcome.

A few more stops — to gaze, to take a short walk in the forest, or to throw a few rocks as far as I could into the Bow River just because I'm a boy — and I reached the end of the Bow Valley Parkway. A sign pointed up to the famous Lake Louise ski area, and I crossed the main highway and drove towards Chateau Lake Louise. Along the way I noticed a sign to the old station, so I took a detour. The lovely old log building at the side of the tracks was the old Laggan Station, but today it bears the name Lake Louise. Two old rail cars sat beyond the building, one restored and used as an occasional dining car.

It was here that Lady Agnes Macdonald, wife of Canada's Prime Minister Sir John A. Macdonald, scored a gutsy point for the fairer sex. It seems she'd been admiring the huge steam locomotive waiting to pull her train over the mountains. A "monster" she said, "necessary for the steep grades both ascending and descending, over which we have to go." Not wanting to miss a glimpse of the remarkable scenery, she rode on the cowcatcher of engine No. 374 from Lake Louise to the coast. Her husband thought her scheme ridiculous and possibly dangerous, but she had her way, tucked around from waist to foot in a linen carriage-cover and accompanied by a railroad superintendent, who was far less enthusiastic about it than she was. Sir John, preferring the company and liquid refreshment of the lounge car, stayed inside. During the trip she was, in her own words:

> Breathless — almost awestricken — but with a wild triumph in my heart, I look from farthest mountain peak, lifted high above me, to the shining pebbles at my feet! Warm wind rushes past; a thousand sunshine colours dance in the air…. There is a glory of brightness and beauty everywhere, and I laugh aloud on the cowcatcher, just because it is so delightful!

All was quiet on the line that day. I walked the length of the platform, then turned back and entered the old station, now an attractive restaurant gloriously a-clutter with artifacts and mementos. I was tempted to have a very late lunch, but I didn't. The sky was darkly threatening again, and I had miles to go before I slept. Well, about three miles, actually, but they were all uphill.

Location, location, location — the three vital elements of real estate, and effective back scratching. Chateau Lake Louise has location in spades and simply could not sit any prettier.

Tom Wilson, a CPR employee who ferried supplies to the crews working at Kicking Horse Pass, became the first non-native person to see the wondrous sight of Lake Louise. Following the sound of thundering avalanches on a rainy day in August, 1882, he came looking for the "Lake of Little Fishes," a place he'd heard about from Edwin Hunter, a member of the local Stoney band. He liked what he found:

> As God is my judge I never in all my explorations saw such a matchless scene. The surface of the lake was still as a mirror. On the right and left, forests that had never known the axe came down to the shores, apparently growing out of the blue and green water.

Wilson named it Emerald Lake, though it was also known as Laggan Lake, being close to the CPR's Laggan Station, itself named after a village in Inverness-shire, Scotland. He returned two years later to see a clear blue sky reflected in the water; realizing that Emerald wasn't suitable, he renamed the lake Louise after a woman in the party he was then guiding from the station up into the mountains. The Geographical Society of Canada officially adopted the name, but they claimed it was for Queen Victoria's fourth daughter.

William Van Horne, scouting for CPR hotel locations, also liked the beauty spot, and in 1890 a single-storey log cabin, about forty-five feet long by thirty feet wide, was built here on a thousand-year-old mound of glacial deposit. Apart from a central area serving as bar, dining room and gathering place, the cabin had two bedrooms and a kitchen.

For three years, CPR prose lured visitors to the remote chalet:

> This quiet resting place in the mountains situated on the margin of Lake Louise, about two miles distant from the station at Laggan from which there is a good carriage drive, is an excellent vantage point for tourists and explorers desiring to see the lakes and the adjacent scenery at their leisure. The rates are $2.50 per day.

An excellent vantage point it was, but not without its problems, as one visitor pointed out: "The road there is atrocious and the mosquitoes at the house on the lake beyond any I ever saw...life is a burden there."

On June 19, 1893, the chalet burned down, and the $2,500 from insurance was all the CPR would spend on replacing it. However, that budget bought a two-storey cabin built farther back from the lake that could accommodate up to twenty guests. Improvements were ongoing and expansion seemed imminent. Thomas Sorby came in to enlarge the building but before the end of that century the place was obsolete, and the CPR brought in Francis Mawson Rattenbury, between 1900 and 1912, to overhaul the whole affair. The chalet grew, and grew, with three-storey extensions, then wings and dormers, until a large neo-Tudor hotel stood on the site. And still guests were being turned away for lack of space.

The Swiss mountain styling of Chateau Lake Louise is completed by a couple of silent eavesdroppers, mounted over the pay phones. Photo: Dave Preston

In 1912, Walter S. Painter, having spent half a dozen years on a new design for the Lake Louise hotel, came up with a large concrete annex, which would adjoin the Rattenbury building and add more than three hundred rooms. The style didn't seem to draw from French chateaux, Scottish baronial or anything the CPR had built before, and while it wasn't ugly, it seemed destined to be a hotel to look from, not at.

To cope with extra visitor traffic, and to help supply the construction materials, a narrow gauge railway was built from Laggan Station three and a half miles up to the hotel. As well as hauling lumber and furniture, the modest locomotive pulled up to 180 passengers at a time, for a fare of fifty cents per ride. During its first year of operation, 32,500 guests used the little train, which had a turntable at either end of its run.

The twenties came, bringing with them affluence and roaring trade, and a stroke of bad luck. You've probably detected something of a pattern regarding early Canadian hotels and fires, and the Chateau Lake Louise had more than its share. On July 3, 1924, the following telegraph tickered in to Grant Hall, the CPR headquarters in Montreal: "Chalet Lake Louise Hotel on fire and am advised beyond control — 2:38 pm C. Murphy."

Smoke emerged from the third-storey staff quarters in the North Wing as metal fire screens were quickly lowered to seal off the Painter wing from the burning Rattenbury hotel. Canvas fire hoses had been put away wet, apparently, and had quietly rotted away on the reels. Firefighters, hampered by such faulty equipment, struggled to keep the blaze under control and damage was considerable. The staff lost all their posessions, because, according to one worker who helped fight the fire, "our guests' and the Company's property were the primary consideration from the outset." Before nightfall, the whole of the wooden Rattenbury building was gone.

Entertainment types rally to the cry of "the show must go on," but time and again the hospitality industry demonstrates uninterruptable service under duress. Within hours, dinner was being served for 126 guests, with the usual orchestra and dancing from nine until eleven. Next day, valet, shoe shine and hairdressing were all operating as normal. (Will there be anything else, sir?)

Construction of a replacement building by architects Barott and Blackader of Montreal began almost immediately. The small railway earned its fuel, carrying more than 26,000 tons of materials and supplies to the site. A shell of wooden boards over a steel frame, covered by tar paper, protected crews so that building could continue through the winter. It was well below freezing outside, but steam pipes within the shell raised the temperature to a workable forty-five degrees Fahrenheit.

The following summer, having dropped the word Chalet from its title, the CPR proclaimed the new, fireproof concrete building was "The largest and most modern equipped chateau in the world." For the grand opening on June 1, 1925, a special train brought 350 tons of foodstuffs from a CPR supply farm at Strathmore, Alberta. The new pantries were stuffed with seven thousand eggs, three hundred sacks of flour, three thousand pounds of butter, twenty tons of sugar, eleven thousand pounds of turkey, eight thousand pounds of roasting fowl, eighteen whole lambs and a dozen hogs. Company's coming, indeed.

I swung the rental car around to the front entrance of the chateau and joined a line of several other vehicles. Busy time. Being 5,500 feet or so above sea level the atmosphere was cool and thin, and thanks to the bellmen, somewhat European. They bustled around in heavy green mountaineering jackets, with Austrian-style hats in black felt, and short, black plus-fours, heavy socks and hiking boots. Van Horne's

vision of turning this into the New World's equivalent of the Swiss Alps was still being realized. One ruddy-faced youth greeted me with steaming breath and parked my car; another helped me into the lobby with my luggage.

The lobby is a grand affair. Graceful arches, three of which form the front desk, reach upwards of twelve feet to the mezzanine level. A heavy oak staircase with fat bannisters rises from the centre of one side, parting halfway to fork around a

The views from the dining room at Lake Louise make it hard to keep your eyes on the food. Photo: Dave Preston

central display area where a bronze statue, *Children of Yesterday* by Vilem Zach, sits. It's a life-size replica of a native woman and two children, one of which she carries on her back. I later learned it could have been mine for $75,000.

A bellhop escorted me to room 819, a fabulous penthouse suite in one of the towers with a spectacular view of the lake. Victoria Mountain rose magnificently before me, to about 10,000 feet, capped by a thick, pristine slab of white glacier. To the right and left, just as Tom Wilson said, bristling slopes of forest came right down to the aquamarine water. It was one heaven of a view, and I had about 170 degrees of it. I tried hard to believe I deserved such a treat.

The suite wasn't too shabby, either. It was huge, with two couches, two coffee tables, a table-cum-desk, four upholstered wingback armchairs, a large TV and separate minibar. A fireplace with a wooden mantelpiece was featured along one wall and two large chandeliers hung from polished wooden panels in the ceiling. The two walls without windows were tastefully appointed with prints of wildlife and landscapes, one dated 1885. The carpet, a plain blue-green, matched the lake.

During my first exploratory tour of the hotel I heard an announcement coming through speakers in the hallway ceilings, telling me there was going to be a fire drill and not to worry, so I didn't. The announcements continued, some live and some recorded, as I took the elevator (which you should never do during a real fire, of course) down to the lobby and continued my walk, all the while hearing a loud bell that turned the heads of quite a few visitors — mainly, I suspect, those who didn't speak English. Five minutes later a cheerful announcement told us the drill had finished, and the bell stopped.

I spotted a working Cutler mail system, and peered down a Germanic white hallway lined with iron sconces, where mounted deer heads grinned down at me. Nearby I found the Chateau Deli, with a variety of hot and cold snacks and a cafeteria-style eating area, and next to that the Walliser Stube, or wine bar, closed until early evening.

Downstairs I toured the shopping corridor and saw clothes, jewellery and lots of Christmasy things for sale. Why not? It looked like Christmas everywhere but on the calendar, where it looked like September 30. In the art gallery there was work by Canadian artists, ranging in price from $400 to $18,000. Inuit work, according to the young sales clerk, was by far the most popular, but I saw nothing that would fit my budget or luggage space.

Just off the lobby I found a climate-controlled glass case displaying a vertical collection of Château Mouton Rothschild wines, from 1945 to 1994. Baron Philippe de Rothschild began the practice of commissioning one-of-a-kind labels each year, designed by famous artists such as Pablo Picasso, Andy Warhol, Marc Chagall and Henry Moore.

At the top of a plush, red staircase at the west end of the lower level I discovered the Victoria dining room. It was closed until later in the evening, but I took a look around and admired its painted ceiling beams, Swiss murals and tables crisp with white linen. Again, the view out over the lake was fabulous. At the other end of the hotel I found the famous Edelweiss Dining Room, beautifully appointed and with an aesthetic charm that extended to the patrons by means of a semi-formal dress code.

A CPR brochure from around 1930 says of the hotel:
Chateau evenings have the sparkle of a smart club on gala nights. Beautiful evening gowns trail down broad stairs and through the luxurious lounges. Distinguished-looking groups laugh and chat in a fascinating variety of tongues... the ballroom opening off the main lounge is a place of soft colours, deep chairs, palms, and the wooing rhythms of a sophisticated five-piece orchestra.

But I found only the wooing rhythms of Sebastian at the zither, a man who sat at the end of the lobby, playing a series of well-known tunes and selling CDs to visitors.

Since I'd done laundry at Banff, I would be able to make

myself a little more distinguished looking for dinner. Before dressing up, however, I'd promised myself to undress for a swim. The lake was only slightly warmer than the glacier melting into it, and the outdoor pool had been filled in long ago. It now housed an art gallery (though I later learned there are plans to re-open it, under cover of a roof). So I followed signs to the rear bowels of the building and finally found an indoor place to swim. The pool was quiet, about thirty-six feet long and twenty feet wide, and no diving, please. I shared it for a while with two small children and their mother. After I'd done a few dozen laps the family left and I threw myself into the large hot tub, where I splashed and flailed and amused myself in all sorts of carefree aquatic ways...until I realized I was being watched from the upstairs co-ed exercise room that looks out onto the pool area.

For some reason, dinner became a makeshift meal from the deli, after which I went outside for a walk. By eight o'clock the sky was stripped of any blue and I had the lake and its margin virtually to myself. I walked along the edge of the lake for twenty minutes or more, until I reached a point where I could look across and see the hotel lights shimmering on the inky black water. The air was bitterly cold and promising to snow. Walking back to the hotel I saw people inside in the various rooms, bars and restaurants; it was like watching a movie with the sound turned off. I looked up to my penthouse suite and saw the lights I'd left on and felt good, privileged even, knowing I could ride up there in an elevator and sleep the velvety sleep of a prince in such luxury. I also felt a twinge of sadness that I was alone and had no one to entertain in the suite, no one to show off the view to, no one with whom I could share a bottle of wine. Over the years I've been poor and surrounded by friends, and fleetingly affluent and alone. And I know which really stinks.

Crossing the lobby en route to the elevator, passing the lobby bar, I caught sight of a familiar face, a man from Oxfordshire whom I'd met on the train from Toronto to

Winnipeg. He saw me, broke into a huge grin, nudged his wife and the pair of them frantically waved me over. Drinks flowed and tales of the intervening days were swapped. It seems we were all in need of company and good cheer, and we filled our hearts with it.

At around eleven o'clock we bid each other farewell and I returned to my suite. I sat for a while watching the snow fall by the window and felt suddenly Christmasy, then suddenly alone again and very far from home. I flicked on the TV and soon realized that a soft pillow held more attraction for me.

I awoke at six the next morning and went through to the living room to see if there was a dawn to look at, but I was too early. The night's quiet snowfall had covered the whole property to a depth of two or three inches and it made a pretty picture — one I thought about capturing on film but didn't. I often think that you can truly experience a special moment or try to record it, but you'll never really do both. Besides, I couldn't be bothered to dig out the camera and set up a tripod and all that stuff, so I just experienced. A solitary woman, wearing a light woollen hat and dark fur coat, walked from the hotel's front door down to the water's edge and left a set of dark prints in the virgin snow. It was a beautiful scene and I had a perfect vantage point. A moment later a thin blue flash from her camera shot out across the water. I went back to bed, and when I got up again a little before eight the place was buzzing with people and all the walkways were darkened and wet from a thousand rushing footprints.

I spent a luxurious chunk of the morning playing in the bathroom with a deep whirlpool bath. Feeling the need to indulge in a bubble bath, I poured two small bottles of shampoo into the tub and turned on the jets. The bathroom filled with a light, airy foam, much more welcoming than the flat, wet white stuff outside. I had a good, long soak and thoroughly pampered myself with smelly soaps, lotions, creams and a rather nice bottle of mouthwash.

It snowed, on and off, all day and the mountains came and

went, in turn clad in torn, foggy shrouds, large cotton candy clouds and slow-moving banks of grey mist. Victoria glacier blazed a brilliant white in sunshine one minute, then was gone the next. Robbed of the view I looked down, and watched a raucous group of Japanese men roll big snowballs and argue about the best way to build a snowman, their wives and girlfriends photographing every move and gesture.

I took the car around to Moraine Lake, a scenic, fifteen-minute drive from the hotel, where I mingled with a busload of British tourists and looked at the still, grey waters. A couple of hardy canoeists disappeared slowly but purposefully into the far gloom, as though no one should ever see them again. The lake sits about 6,500 feet above sea level, and it's frigid, so I warmed myself in the bright, cheerful gift shop and, like every one of the British tourists, I fondled all the goods but didn't buy a thing.

I returned to the hotel by late afternoon, and walked past the Glacier Saloon as I'd done several times during my walk-about tours of the hotel, but this time I turned back and went inside, looking for supper. The bar, though billed as a western-style saloon, seemed a bit confused about its identity. The furniture was dark and heavy, with brass rails and lamps strewn around, but rap music throbbed out of speakers, then reggae, and all the while a hockey game pulled my attention to the numerous TV screens. Hardly the rustic pioneer watering hole I expected.

However, I played along and had the Round-Up Stew — a hearty concoction of buffalo and venison, carrots, potatoes, peppers and dark gravy. It came with a tea-biscuit — a crumbly, unsweetened scone. Dang me but it was good! I washed it down with a pint of Big Rock beer and gol-darned the fact that I had no bandana to wipe my brow, lasso to fidget with, harmonica to play, or any of the other cowboy things with which to set a spell, or whatever.

On Saturday morning I awoke at seven to another white panoply outside my window. As I ate breakfast downstairs, I heard that the road to Jasper wasn't so good after all the

snow, so I planned to have one last good look at the view, then check out of this Swissness and drive carefully north to catch a train.

One thing the motorist learns very quickly while driving in Canada's parks is that if a couple or more vehicles are pulled over to the side of the highway it's unlikely to be an accident or breakdown. Usually it's because there's important wildlife to be looked at and photographed. So, when I came upon some vans pulled over and a group of people gathered in a clearing just down the bank to my right, I slowed down and reached for my camera, ready to snap a bear, wolf, extra-large bug, or whatever the attraction turned out to be. As I approached, however, I realized it was a guided nature walk, with a guy holding up a piece of bark and explaining its wonder to his congregation. Not worth a frame of mine, so I sped up and continued to Jasper.

It might have been cold outside but in the Chevy it was toasty warm, and bright sunlight suddenly appeared to make the mountains even larger than big-enough life. The song on the radio was good enough to sing, dance and drive to. So I did. Minutes flashed by like seconds and before long I saw a big white sign to my right: British Columbia. I smiled — it's my home province after all — but then I spoiled the mood by thinking. Lake Louise and Jasper are both in Alberta, and that's where I should have been. I should not have been crossing the border yet, and certainly not by road. Almost immediately I saw another sign saying Great Divide. I became more concerned. I didn't notice all this on the drive down from Jasper so how come it was here now? Because I was in Yoho National Park, that's how come.

National parks people work hard at blending the hardware of civilization into the natural landscape. Signs, for instance, are brown, and not as glaring or clear as the green ones you'll see elsewhere on Canadian highways. Brown

signs blend in quite nicely, especially if you're singing loudly and paying more attention to the sky, the mountains and the wildlife than you are to the signs. I'd missed my turnoff for the Jasper road. Some might say I've spent a lifetime overstepping the mark, but it's not every day you get the chance to overstep one as big as this. I decided to go and see the Great Divide for myself.

Yoho comes from the Cree word meaning awe, and about three-quarters of a million people a year come to see this, the second-smallest of the Rocky Mountain parks at just over five hundred square miles. I calculated I had three minutes to explore it if I was to get back to Jasper in time for the train.

Many minutes later, I finally arrived at a large wooden archway. It said British Columbia on one side and Alberta on the other. This was it. The Great Divide. A major provincial border and a topographical summit, from which all waterways flow either east or west. Tiny meltwater brooks and spring-fed streams beginning at the continental divide have a long way to go to the oceans, whether they go east to the Arctic and Atlantic, or west to the Pacific. The rail tracks were just a few yards away, down a footpath and beyond a stone cairn, so I jogged down the path to see the other plaques and monuments.

Back on the highway I hit the speed limit, or a little more, as soon as possible. Several minutes later I saw the same nature group, in about the same spot, which was where I should have made a right turn to Jasper. I made the turn and checked my watch. I was okay, just, if things went well, but a large yellow sign to my right was indicating current road conditions. It had four options: Good, Fair, Poor and Closed. The marker pointed to Poor and I felt my heart inch a little closer to my stomach.

I reached a toll booth where a Parks Canada employee asked if I had a pass for the park. I said yes, explaining that I bought one as I left Jasper. He needed the receipt, which was in a loose bundle in my luggage along with a thousand others I'd amassed on my journey, so I pulled out fistfuls of paper

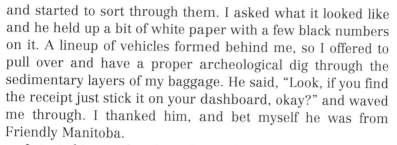

and started to sort through them. I asked what it looked like and he held up a bit of white paper with a few black numbers on it. A lineup of vehicles formed behind me, so I offered to pull over and have a proper archeological dig through the sedimentary layers of my baggage. He said, "Look, if you find the receipt just stick it on your dashboard, okay?" and waved me through. I thanked him, and bet myself he was from Friendly Manitoba.

I started to wonder about the road conditions, and wonder turned to worry when I saw a snowplough coming towards me. It had obviously been working. I knew I was tight for time so I drove as fast as I dared, within reason and almost within speed limits.

The road trip, apart from a little anxiety, was a splendid one and the mountains were glorious. I pulled over to look at a huge landslide that occurred many years ago, the large boulders still piled up by the roadside, and I could see the trail of well-aged destruction leading back up the mountain. I got out, ran back down the shoulder about fifty yards to take a picture, then ran to the car. I pulled at the driver's door handle and it didn't budge. It was locked. The keys were in the ignition. The car had central locking. I was in the middle of nowhere and traffic, once light, was now non-existent. Cold as the air was, I began to perspire. My armpits prickled and a thousand thoughts flashed through my mind, all of them horrible. There wasn't another train out of Jasper for two days. Once again I realized why my mother, having given me life forty-odd winters ago, still worries about me. I circled the car, ranting like a man possessed, and on one circuit I tried the passenger side door. It opened! A miracle! I reached across and snatched the keys out of the ignition before they were spirited away by the evil force that was trying to scupper my trip. Back in the driver's seat I vowed, loudly, never again to get out of the car and leave the keys in. And I also thanked GM for making at least one vehicle with a faulty central locking system.

Rushed as I was, nothing spoiled my enjoyment of the

Icefields Parkway. What a fabulous road it is, whatever the weather. I was using a lot of film, more than elsewhere in the journey. Manitoba might be friendly but it doesn't smile for the camera as much as western Alberta. On a clear day, they say, you can see almost twenty glaciers from the road between Banff and Jasper. I never tired of gazing up at their bright ledges and wanting, if just for a moment, to walk a little way on that ancient ice. In a world dominated by electronic communication and entertainment, it's magnificent to escape the marks of commerce and look upon nature, pure and simple. I wondered, cynically, how long it might be before these glaciers and mountains, which attract the gaze of millions, would be franchised. I imagined bright corporate logos in shocking primary colours projected onto the white backdrop of these snow-capped ranges from a satellite. "This view brought to you by the Arrogance R Us Corporation" or some such. Is there any place on earth we cannot soil with our avarice? I hope so.

I zoomed into Jasper and saw the train standing in the station, and well past it. I couldn't find a place to park the rental car so I circled around for precious minutes wondering when I'd see the train move, slowly but positively, in the direction of Vancouver. I finally found a spot, purged the debris of my road trip and rushed my baggage into the station. I caught the eye of Lydia at the car rental counter, she took my keys, and I recited the mileage and signed some paperwork. I thanked her and pressed into her hand a fancy chocolate in a dark green cardboard envelope that was left on my pillow at the Chateau Lake Louise. We exchanged smiles and goodbyes and I strode out onto the platform.

I realized the train wasn't about to move when I spotted the engineer coming back from a fast food place with his hands full of burger and fries. I walked over to meet him, introduced myself, and seconds later we were sitting up in the cab chatting. Shawn had been driving trains for twenty years, and judging by the way he was tackling the fries he'd been fasting for just as long. The other engineer, Trevor, joined us

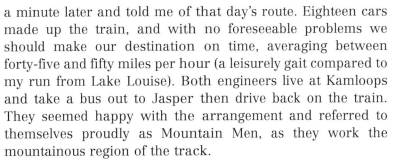
a minute later and told me of that day's route. Eighteen cars made up the train, and with no foreseeable problems we should make our destination on time, averaging between forty-five and fifty miles per hour (a leisurely gait compared to my run from Lake Louise). Both engineers live at Kamloops and take a bus out to Jasper then drive back on the train. They seemed happy with the arrangement and referred to themselves proudly as Mountain Men, as they work the mountainous region of the track.

We left Jasper station at exactly 4:25 p.m., as it says on the timetable. Sometimes you can believe all you read.

Jasper
to
Vancouver

THE ELGIN MANOR CAR, ROOM F, TO BE PRECISE, WOULD BE MY home for the next seventeen hours as we rolled over the mountains to the Pacific coast. It was a double room and very comfortable. My VIA attendant, Chris, introduced himself and noticed my briefcase, saying he could provide me with a table if I wanted to work. I said, with well-practised ease, that I didn't want to work, but the table appeared anyway.

I wandered back to the dome car, immediately behind mine, and made myself a cup of Earl Grey tea and brought it back. A quick wash and change of shirts and I felt much better, and pleased to be aboard my penultimate train ride. Three more attempted sleeps, then I'd be home....

By five o'clock, soon after our hot hors d'oeuvres, Chris was parading a tray of sparkling white wine and I partook, along with all my fellow passengers in the lower level of the dome car. Our little band comprised two women from Toronto, a male friend of theirs from Kitchener, and a couple from Georgia, Alabama. One of the Toronto women asked where I was from, and when I said Vancouver Island she barked, "What's wrong with your tamaracks?" It floored me for a moment, then I remembered they're trees. She followed up with a question about arbutus and I changed the subject.

A young couple in brown VIA golf shirts entered the car and introduced themselves. They were Keith and Allyson and

they were our guides, or Activity Coordinators. It was their job to make sure we had fun and saw whatever there was to see along the way. They would tell us, in person or by a PA announcement, when we were coming up to a point of interest, such as Moose Lake, which Allyson duly announced. It's eight kilometres long, she said, and the woman from Georgia asked how far that was in miles. Allyson said one point eight, and surprisingly the woman seemed happy enough with the answer. Allyson was twenty years old and although her math was suspect she spoke three languages fluently, she said, and had a few words in others. A party of four Asians came through the car just after she told us that and she greeted them in Japanese. The guy at the front walked past her and said bitterly, "We're not Japanese, we're from Taiwan." Canadians abroad hate being called Americans, so he got my sympathy. Allyson shrugged, kept smiling and let her green eyes say a small Whoops.

My companions had enjoyed the trip so far and had good things to say about train travel. "It's like a hotel but you've got more chance to meet people." By now, some of them had been on the same train for two full days and nights, so they knew each other and made frequent reference to private jokes and running gags.

Another major point of interest came up as we forged towards the heart of the Rockies: Yellowhead Pass. Three men have been erroneously cited as being the "yellow headed" fur trader that the pass and community of Tête Jaune Cache were named after: Jasper Hawes, Francois Decoigne, and Pierre Hatsinaton. Actually, it was Pierre Bostonais, a mixed-blood Iroquois who worked for both the Hudson's Bay and the North West companies, and who was killed in the upper Peace River region in 1827. (It was also known to pioneers as Leather Pass, Cowdung Pass, Jasper Pass, Jasper House Pass, Tête Jaune Passe, and Rocky Mountain Pass.)

Sandford Fleming failed in the 1880s to persuade the CPR to follow the Yellowhead Pass route, cutting though the Rockies at an elevation of just over 3,600 feet, but both the

Another mountain, another lake, as The Canadian *takes the scenic route to Vancouver.* Photo: Dave Preston

Grand Trunk Pacific and the Canadian Northern railways ultimately chose it for their lines.

Rumbling slowly through the pass we came into Mount Robson Park, crossing a provincial border and a time zone into the deal. Nice as it was to finally be in British Columbia, I'd had a good time in Alberta so I didn't hurry to turn my watch back.

Lesley, another VIA attendant, came through the car with another bottle of "champagne" for refills, and she received plenty of attention. At 5:30 p.m. we heard the first call for dinner and I took a seat in the dining car opposite a couple from Ladysmith, Vancouver Island. They were originally from Brandon, Manitoba, and seemed to miss absolutely nothing about the place, especially the weather, but they'd been back to visit family. They were the first people I'd met on *The Canadian* who seemed to be using it as non-vacational transport.

My dinner began with the Hot and Sour Soup, which was

good, and I rinsed away the stress of a day spent driving too quickly on snow-covered mountain roads with a glass of Sauvignon Blanc. I followed this with an excellent Chicken with Apricot Stuffing, but I should have had the beef for old times' sake. Let me explain.

On July 20, 1871, British Columbia was admitted to the Dominion of Canada. One of the conditions of entry is that the dominion government should, within two years, start building a railway from the Pacific towards the Rocky Mountains, and from a point east of the Rocky Mountains towards the Pacific to connect the seaboard of British Columbia with a national railway system. In return, the new province would grant "in trust" a twenty-mile-wide belt on either side of the proposed line, for which it would receive $100,000 per annum in perpetuity. Ranchers in the Thompson-Okanagan district, who had watched their markets in the Cariboo goldfields dwindle to almost nothing, saw the railway as the answer to their dreams. Not only would construction require huge quantities of beef and other produce to feed workers, but the completed railway would provide access to the meat-hungry markets of eastern Canada.

Sandford Fleming, the engineer in charge, was greeted extravagantly as he and his party of surveyors travelled through this area. During the summer of 1881, railway construction was expected to employ about five thousand men, so the CPR invited tenders for the supply of fresh beef to feed them. The demand was so great that only the largest ranches could consider offering cattle. It became obvious that the following year would be even better, and that all available cattle from the Thompson-Okanagan would be required to supply the market. Enter Joseph Blackbourne Greaves, who smelled the char-broiled potential for a beefy dollar. A crafty syndicate formed and began quietly purchasing all available cattle in the region. The price climbed steadily but the CPR paid, and eventually the syndicate controlled the market and prospered, buying land and forming the Douglas Lake Cattle Company, the largest ranch ever known in the British Commonwealth.

We were travelling alongside but high above a small river to our right, and the tree-covered hills led up to mountains in the distance. Except for the railway, there was little sign of civilization of any kind. Word came down the train that someone saw a moose some way back along the track, and this was followed by a gentle chorus of Oohs and Aahs and faces turned with renewed interest to the windows. The trackside telegraph wires dipped and dove down towards thick bushes, and some poles were twisted, bent, leaning or snapped off. Some of the wires were extremely taut because of fallen trees and branches, but they were not, I presumed, in use, or as vital as they were a few decades ago. In 1969, the CPR hired helicopters to blow heavy frost and snowdrifts off the wires in B.C. when track crews and snowploughs could not get through. That's expensive snow removal.

We began to pass Mount Robson, and it took a while. It's the highest peak in the B.C. Rockies and looked every inch the part, its massive bulk sitting majestically at the east end of a broad, well-treed valley. The summit was just visible, but it was partially shrouded by blowing snow and streaking wisps of cloud.

I recalled another record for this region. In March, 1939, a six-year-old bull terrier named Betty Lou claimed the world "Canine Railway Travel Award" for having ridden more than 400,000 miles along this stretch of track (more than seven hundred round-trips) between Jasper and Kamloops. She was kept hidden by CNR baggage man Bill Wocks, who worked on this run, and both were fed by telegraph agents, the only people who knew about the illicit dog.

As daylight faded we forged along the broad valley between the Rockies and the Columbia Mountains, and I joined a car full of other diners for the first sitting of dinner. We passed Lempriere, which didn't seem to have much going for it, and as seating in the dome thinned out, I went to watch the sun fall to its death across the North Thompson River. Unlike the lazy dawn fire that burns up from a prairie horizon, or the lin-

The dome car gets a regular wash to make sure scenic beauty isn't lost on peering passengers. Photo: Dave Preston

gering golden orb that sinks, oh, so slowly into the ocean, mountain sunrises and sunsets don't mess about. They're here and gone. All was darkness by seven o'clock.

I changed my watch to Pacific Time, the time zone I lived in, and immediately felt closer to home. We would follow rivers until we reached Vancouver. First the North Thompson, then South Thompson, and finally the mighty Fraser with its notorious canyon. The terrain we rolled through would gradually change from arid desert to lush green and finally coastal delta, but most would pass in darkness. Had we left Toronto twelve hours later, at 11:00 p.m. instead of in the morning, we might have enjoyed the full splendour of these coastal mountains. But that would have meant boarding the train at Jasper at around three in the morning, which really isn't that appealing. (The Rocky Mountaineer, a train run by a private company, capitalizes on this scenery and runs sightseers from Vancouver to Kamloops and back during daylight.)

I took another walk up and down the train, but all was

quiet. I heard an employee's radio say "Ten minutes to Clearwater, on the right." There were two women chatting about alarm systems in the rear park car, but all the dome cars were now empty, as was the bar. I recognized a painting as I walked past, and realized the train had made a couple of complete trans-Canadian runs since I saw it last. It was apparent that no large British tour groups were on board, as the bar would have been full, smoky and rollicking by now.

We stopped at Clearwater, where nothing seemed to happen, and we pulled away slowly from the dinging bell of a road crossing. I walked all the way to the front of the train, checking each dome car for possible company, but it was now obvious — everyone except a few staff had gone to bed. Nine forty-five on Saturday night. What a wild bunch. I mused about the idea of VIA running a mobile health farm, or a linear Betty Ford Clinic.

Some time after eleven we pulled into Kamloops. It was once a busy rail intersection, but the relatively new suburban station is far from downtown and was almost deserted. I saw only a sodium glare cutting through the darkness. The old railway station, the one I happened upon earlier in the summer, freshly renovated and with its new neighbourhood of apartment buildings, sees no passenger train.

On the way back to my room I approached an older couple in a section; they were both in bed but hadn't pulled down the curtain so they were on display for all to see. She was cosily tucked up with flannelette and slick with cold cream, trying to sleep, and he was lying there in red plaid pajamas, smiling away and drumming his fingers on the blanket over his chest. Maybe he was claustrophobic. Or maybe he wasn't used to going to bed this early. We smiled and nodded to each other as I brushed passed.

I turned off all the lights in my room and lay on the bed, looking out at the night. It was clear and stars were out in their millions. I switched the bedding around, so that I could lie with my head by the window. I saw the odd light of a cabin, and the occasional dim blue glow from a living room TV, but mostly it was dark on the ground and milky white in the sky. I saw the shooting star I'd been looking for, and a few minutes later there was another. I pressed my face against the cold glass and tried to spot the mileposts as they flashed by in the gloom. I was waiting for the train to cross the scene of the Last Spike. Not the famous one, driven into a CP railroad tie in Craigellachie on November 7, 1885, by the hugely bearded Donald Smith and his important entourage. Nor the second one, driven into the Grand Trunk Pacific at Fort Fraser on April 7, 1914. The spike scene I was about to ride over, or had just ridden over, was the one that completed the third transcontinental railroad of this wide country — the Canadian Northern Pacific line. You're forgiven for not knowing about it. The ceremony, if it merits that title, was a brief occasion carried out by a few workmen and engineers on January 23, 1915, at Mile 62. Somewhere out there, across the river by the side of the Trans-Canada Highway a few miles south of Ashcroft, was a plaque. That's all. You can't even buy a T-shirt to say you've been there.

I couldn't sleep. The stars were intensely bright and distracting, and I couldn't bring myself to draw the blind on such a wondrous sky. I got a real sense of being alone. There was room in the night for a ghost story, so I'll give you one. Once upon a time, right there on that very piece of lonely track I was rolling over, a major railway disaster was averted by some mysterious power. On New Year's Eve, 1924, the predecessor of my train, the westbound *Trans Canada Limited*, was steaming along at a hectic rate trying to make up lost time. As it sped towards Toketic at Mile 64, the fireman and engineer both heard two distinct whistles being sounded from the communication cord, which meant the conductor wanted to stop at the next station. So they dutifully slowed down and stopped just before Pukaist Creek Bridge, only to be severely questioned by the conductor as to why, since they were damned late to begin with and he certainly hadn't requested the stop. Releasing the brake and getting underway again, they suddenly noticed a locomotive on the track right ahead of them, unlit and almost hidden by clouds of steam. They quickly braked again and went to investigate. The phantom locomotive was supposed to wait on a siding for the passenger train to pass, but the crew had fallen asleep and the train had started forward by itself. Had that two-whistle signal not been given, the trains would have met in a high-speed head-on collision on the bridge.

Incidentally, the term "runaway train," which we've embraced for more than a century in language and culture, has been officially dropped by the rail industry. They're now called uncontrolled movement occurrences. And I'll bet they don't get nearly as many mentions in songs.

Another incident on this same stretch of track had a less fortunate outcome. In the 1970s, a freight train travelling at night hit a rockslide and two crew members were killed. They left us the legacy of ditch lights, which were henceforth installed on all Canadian trains. I pressed my face to the window and each time the train made a bend to the right I could see those ditch lights now, sweeping darkness away from the trackside.

At some small, late hour we rolled into another garish sodium glare, possibly Boston Bar, so I pulled down the blind and tucked myself in. I didn't sleep well, or for more than ten minutes at a stretch, so the grey light of pre-dawn didn't catch me off-guard and I watched it slowly warm, from grey to pink, then apricot. I recalled that breakfast might end at 8:00 a.m. if we were on time so I dragged myself out of bed and made myself presentable.

Tucking into my usual train breakfast — *The Canadian*: two eggs over easy, bacon, hash browns, brown toast, orange juice and tea with milk (not the cream that's always offered in a small white jug) — I and a couple of American women watched the sun come fully up, a bright orange yolk bobbing over the horizon to our left.

A VIA attendant came by and whispered that it was someone's birthday and pointed to an older woman sitting at the

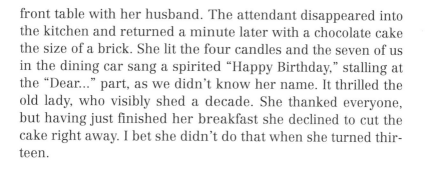

front table with her husband. The attendant disappeared into the kitchen and returned a minute later with a chocolate cake the size of a brick. She lit the four candles and the seven of us in the dining car sang a spirited "Happy Birthday," stalling at the "Dear..." part, as we didn't know her name. It thrilled the old lady, who visibly shed a decade. She thanked everyone, but having just finished her breakfast she declined to cut the cake right away. I bet she didn't do that when she turned thirteen.

A bright morning filled the sky, and we were nearing the end of our line. The Pacific Terminus of the railway, from 1883 until 1887, was Port Moody, where the first train ever to travel from Canadian sea to sea arrived on November 8, 1885. Two weeks later, the first through freight train steamed in, carrying several hundred barrels of oil destined for the Royal Navy at Esquimalt, on Vancouver Island.

Unfortunately, Port Moody's shallow harbour and scruffy population of squatters and speculators made it less than ideal, so the line was pushed twelve miles farther west, towards Vancouver proper. The provincial government transferred about six thousand acres of land to the CPR to build a new terminus, near English Bay. The first through train arrived on May 23, 1887, and the young city boomed. During the first decade of the twentieth century, Vancouver's population mushroomed from 26,000 to more than 100,000.

With less than an hour to go before scheduled arrival, I was up in the dome car, which was about three-quarters full. The Sunday morning sun was glorious and I could not see a cloud in the sky, just the dull, brownish atmosphere of Vancouver, dead ahead. *The Canadian* that arrives here on the weekend is often on time, apparently, because there are fewer freight trains running. We passed beneath several urban bridges and saw evidence of the city's homeless. A mattress here, and an old couch there, a smothering carpet of old plastic bags and garbage. Conversation in the dome car turned to street people and a comparison of the problem in American and Canadian societies. Turns out it seemed to be about the same, and no one had an answer. We slowed to walking pace for the next bridge, and saw a large bundle wrapped in a dusty, soiled blanket. It was a person sleeping. At least we silently hoped they were sleeping, and conversation died for several seconds.

Minutes later we pulled to a halt next to a freight train beside some industrial yards, each fiercely protected by razor wire and filled with buildings bizarrely coloured by graffiti. I couldn't remember hearing much noise from outside the train, apart from the occasional road-crossing bell, but sounds now flooded in from all directions. I saw a Sky Train glide smoothly over a concrete bridge above us, and we started to reverse, going around in a huge arc that led us to Vancouver's Pacific Central Station. We slowed again, and our progress was barely measurable, as if the engineer were docking a space module. The train finally stopped moving at

Dawn chases the train as it finally approaches the west coast.
Photo: Dave Preston

8:55 a.m. precisely. Bang on time, but without a bump or even a nudge. Not bad for a vehicle that had just travelled 2,750 miles in three days.

Why are people so impatient? You must have seen them, standing up before the plane has come to a complete and full stop and grabbing their stuff out of the overhead bins before the captain has turned off the seat-belt signs. They've just been travelling at five hundred miles per hour and must race off at the same speed to the baggage claim area, so they can stand and wait for ten minutes by an empty carousel.

On *The Canadian*, it's all so wonderfully different. The train came to a standstill at Vancouver station, on time, and I gathered up my books, packed my bags and came out of my room, expecting to find passengers crowding the corridor. But it was empty. The others didn't seem to want to leave the train. I was the only one moving and I was certainly in no hurry. Apparently, they all just wanted to sit and chat some more, exchange a few addresses and phone numbers with friends they'd made over the last three days, take a few more photographs and perhaps recount parts of the trans-Canadian adventure they'd just had. And 2,750 miles can make for a lot of recounting.

I bid my farewells and wished a lifetime's luck, then thanked and tipped the VIA staff. I wrangled my luggage out onto the platform and wheeled it down to the station building. It was smaller inside than it looked from along the platform, its apparent grandeur shrunk to a utilitarian space with a brass clock and a few counters. I paused for thought, wanting to remember what it was like having crossed the whole country by train, but I had another ride to make before my journey was really complete so I cut the pause short.

Heading outside to get a cab, I saw a small park right across the street, with a few comatose bodies strewn around its greenery, wrapped in blankets. I turned to look back at

Pacific Central Station and perhaps take a picture. I was moving a little to the right, then left, looking for the best angle, when a man with ancient clothes and a recent facial injury walked over to me and said, "Lost already?" I said I was okay, thanks, and crossed the street with him. He was going to join a few buddies on the grass and carried an alfresco breakfast for them, light on the solids.

While he flipped his aluminum caps, I recalled the last page of CPR's 1887 booklet, *The New Highway to the Orient Across the Mountains, Rivers and Prairies of Canada*:

> No wonder that with all her magnificent resources and precious metals, her coal and iron, her inexhaustible fisheries and vast forests, her delightful climate and rich valleys, her matchless harbours and her newly completed trans-continental railway, British Columbia expects a brilliant future. No wonder that everybody here is at work with all his might!

I took a couple of photos, keeping an eye on my luggage, then crossed back to the taxi stand and hailed the next in line. On the way to the hotel, the driver, hearing that I'd just made a cross-Canada trip, asked if there was a drug problem in

---

Canadian Pacific Railway Station, Vancouver, B.C., circa July to September 1905. Photo: H.W. Gleason, Glenbow Archives NC-53-311

Halifax. I was expecting a comment on the weather, but I recovered enough to say that it wouldn't surprise me if Halifax had a problem, but I certainly didn't create it. He then told me that another cab driver had been held up at knifepoint an hour previously, just two blocks away. He himself had turned down the fare after asking for money up front, which the guy didn't have. The police soon caught the knife-wielding robber, he said, but, like buses, there'd be another one along any minute. Welcome to the not-so-fashionable lower east side.

I'm a country boy, and as pleased as I was to be back on the west coast I'll admit that the itinerary for my twenty-four hours in Vancouver suddenly shrank. I could swim in the hotel, do the art gallery, which is right next door to the hotel, then maybe have dinner. Room service. Ten minutes and almost as many dollars later, I was safely delivered to the Hotel Vancouver. (I knew that other major cities I'd visited probably had just as much street crime, but I'd been fortunate enough to avoid any evidence of it.)

The first Hotel Vancouver opened on May 16, 1887, the year the rail terminus moved to Vancouver from Port Moody and just a week before the first through train from the east arrived at the new station. Though designed by CPR's Thomas Sorby, the original Hotel Vancouver differed greatly from the mountain resorts he'd done for the railway. To be frank, it was a homely affair, four stories high and faced with brick, the roofline dotted with small dormer windows. The CPR also had plans for a grand new opera house, adjoining the hotel, as part of their agreement for land grants within the city. Singers, however, don't pay as much for rooms so work on the opera house was not rushed, and it eventually opened in February, 1891. The railway, of course, brought tremendous growth for the city, and money to build the hotel (and steamship wharfs, and part of the hotel in Banff) came from the lucrative sale of townsite lots. The railway became so embedded in Vancouver that train movements across downtown streets disrupted streetcars and other traffic until 1932, when the Dunsmuir Tunnel was built to connect the CPR station to the rail yard.

Plain as it appeared from the street, the first Hotel Vancouver gave excellent accommodation and service to its guests, offering rooms for three dollars a day and up, with generous discounts for long-term residents. Scrambling to keep up with the enormous demands, the hotel had been entirely rebuilt by the early 1900s, and a whole new structure to replace it was begun in 1913. The second Hotel Vancouver opened in 1916 and was a more elaborate building, sporting a few European lines. It had a grand triple-storey porte-cochère entrance, the extensive Panorama Roof Garden on the sixteenth floor, and a couple of towers.

The third Hotel Vancouver, the one I checked into that day on West Georgia Street, opened in 1939 and is more typical of CPR's chateau style. Its steep copper roof soon became a city landmark, and the stepped parapets and menacing gargoyles added to its mediaeval appeal. Construction began in 1929, but the Depression got in the way of progress and the building remained little more than a steel shell for ten years. During that time, architectural trends changed, and by the time the construction budget reappeared, Art Deco had replaced much of the planned historical, chateau style. Various changes made through the years removed further traces of the original design, but a major renovation, costing $60 million, recently restored many rooms and public areas of the building to their former grandeur.

I arrived by taxi at the covered back entrance, though there are entrances on every side of the hotel, and hauled my luggage through to the lobby. The place was bustling with guests checking out, so I waited my turn and spent the time appreciating a well-polished and fully functional example of the Cutler mail system, of which I'd become quite a fan during the last month. Checking into room 390, a one-bedroom suite, I was impressed by its wonderful old mahogany door, in mar-

vellous condition and set off with bright brass numbers in the old railway hotel style.

Inside, the suite had green carpeting, a burgundy couch and two armchairs, a couple more upholstered chairs and, of course, a large TV. There were two sets of French doors with sheers leading to the bedroom and another TV. A large print in the living room depicted a British rural scene, in the style of Constable; another was a detailed botanical study of a blue flower, *Iris xyphicides* to be exact. The beautiful mahogany desk was far too neat and tidy for me to sully with my books and notes, so I kept them tucked away in my briefcase. The cream walls with beige trim gave the place a restful atmosphere, and I was soon resting in full swing, sprawled across the king-size bed fully clothed.

As usual, I explored the hotel almost immediately. Griffins, the cafe on the lower level, had a lengthy lineup for Sunday brunch, so I steered clear of that and perused the nearby collection of old black and white photographs of the hotel in its three incarnations. To complement these, along the halls off the main lobby hung large, original architectural drawings, in

The first Hotel Vancouver, circa 1887–1889. Photo: Glenbow Archives
NA-387 28

pencil, dated June 5, 1931, and titled "The Canadian National" Hotel at Vancouver.

There were various stores on the main and lower levels and behind the lobby bar was an independently run restaurant with a tempting menu. I was a little early for afternoon tea as advertised at the 900 West Lounge, where I could partake of a selection of sandwiches, fresh-baked scones with Devonshire cream, fruit preserves, and house-made fruit cookies. The preferred house blend was a combination of Ceylon Orange Pekoe and East China Black Tea. One could become quite civilized here in the right company. For a little more money I could enjoy the West Coast Tea, which is salmon in three guises — smoked, candied and cured gravlax — with herb cream cheese and salmon caviar, fruit and nut loaf and bannock bread, followed by seasonal berry crumble.

But enough about food, I had an afternoon to fill with pleasures not of the flesh, for a change. Aside from the Hotel Vancouver, one of the city's best-known buildings is the former Courthouse, dating from 1906. This domed, granite, semi-classical edifice was designed by Francis M. Rattenbury, the architect responsible for the Legislative Buildings and the Empress Hotel in Victoria. It was adapted for use by Vancouver's civic Art Gallery and, handily enough, it was right next door to the hotel and open until supper time.

Since the afternoon was so bright and cheerful, I took the scenic route, crossing the street to take in the diminutive Christ Church Cathedral, opposite the hotel. It remains a major contender for the smallest cathedral I've ever seen, but I'm sure the Good Lord knows that size isn't everything. This is the little church that could and did. Its first congregation was so enthusiastic they held their inaugural service at Christmas, 1888, before the church was even built. Two months later a building committee was formed and an architect chosen — C.O. Wickenden from Winnipeg. The church basement was completed by the fall of 1889, on land bought from the CPR. It looked very much like a root cellar, but it was all that parishioners could afford at the time. The CPR didn't appreciate root cellars toning down its fancy neighbourhood, especially since the almighty railway company was trying to sell adjacent lands, so the building's completion was strongly encouraged. Faith paid off and the required money was raised, the church being built in the Gothic style with ceiling beams of Douglas Fir and windows of beautiful stained glass. A dedication service was held on Sunday, February 17, 1895. Plans to build a bell tower in 1943 were damned by the introduction of new city bylaws carefully designed to prevent such things. In 1971, thoughts turned to making the most of this prime real estate by demolishing the building and incorporating the church into a high-rise complex. The congregation was largely in favour but the community at large was definitely not. Verily, there followed much wailing of the multitudes. A Class A Heritage Building designation in 1976 eventually put paid to such development ideas and placed the cathedral under everlasting protection. Amen.

Having worshipped briefly at the altar of fine architecture, I slipped out of the sunshine and into the cool dark chambers of the art gallery. The printmaking talents of Robert Rauschenberg and the photographic installations of Dominique Blain, not to mention a few colourful daubs by Emily Carr, kept me suitably engaged and away from the city's downtown noise for the rest of the afternoon. The best things in life, we know, are free, but city art galleries still offer damn good value for nearly free, especially to a country boy that doesn't get into town much.

Back at the hotel I swam in the pool for an hour to make sure my appetite was at its peak, then took advice from the concierge and dined three blocks away at a moderately priced restaurant. The food — West Coast Italian, according to the menu — and the service were both top-notch, but the thing that I recall most about the evening's venture was that when I walked back to the hotel at ten o'clock, feeling remarkably safe, most of the stores were still open. People were buying things like shoes, for goodness' sake!

Vancouver
~to~
Victoria

IT FELT AND SMELLED SO GOOD TO BE BACK ON THE WEST COAST. The Maritimes is wonderful, Ontario interesting, Manitoba friendly, and Alberta beautiful, but my dying breaths, I'm sure, will be rich with salty air from the Pacific Ocean. Not being a complete stranger to this neck of the B.C. woods, or the Lower Mainland, as we refer to it around here, it took only a phone call to have an old friend lined up to drive me to the Horseshoe Bay ferry terminal, just north of the city, so I could catch a boat to Vancouver Island.

I caught the 12:30 p.m. sailing aboard the fastest vessel in the B.C. Ferries fleet, the PacifiCat, the second-largest aluminum-hulled catamaran in the world, capable of thirty-seven knots. This ferry could get me over to Departure Bay in Nanaimo in just sixty-five minutes. Remember the word "could."

As soon as I got aboard I did what every ferry passenger does on the west coast — make straight for the cafeteria. It's a phenomenon that always puzzles me. Regardless of the time of day, season or weather conditions, we always feel the immediate need to buy food and drink on the ferry. I stood in line for ten minutes (par for the course) and barely had I got my tea and sandwich when the PA system announced that our sailing time would be about ninety minutes. Slow, I thought, but still plenty of time at the other side to make my 3:15 p.m. train, and the delay came as no surprise to most passengers.

Let's pass the sailing time with an account of why.

These coastal waters used to be serviced by private operators, our CPR friends having been involved since 1901 when
the railway took control of the Hudson's Bay Company's
Canadian Pacific Navigation. CP's sister ships, *Princess
Kathleen* and *Princess Marguerite*, were delivered in 1925
and are still fondly remembered, but their limited capacity
and awkward side-doors were lousy for carrying large numbers of cars and trucks.

Several companies offered ferry services. They had to deal
with three unions and most labour contracts expired toward
the end of 1957; by mid-1958, stymied negotiations brought
marine transportation in the area to a virtual standstill.
Provincial premier of the day, W.A.C. Bennett, stepped in on
July 18, 1958, to announce he'd had enough and that the
British Columbia government would start its own ferry system.

The B.C. Ferry Corporation has been moving passengers
and vehicles across the water with reasonable efficiency ever
since. Then, one December a few years ago, they introduced
the first of three planned catamaran fast-ferries, capable of
carrying 240 vehicles and a thousand passengers. Capable,
that is, when they weren't in for repairs or servicing. Suffice
to say the Fast Cat ferries were a short-lived debacle, with
long-lasting financial effects for the province. My ride aboard
the Pacificat that day has become a collector's item among my
various travel memories.

The ferry docked at Nanaimo a little before two that afternoon and I set off to find the railway station, a task more difficult than I expected. I followed the directions I'd been given
by a ferry worker, but soon got lost. I asked for directions at
least three more times and finally found myself in the right
neighbourhood.

The station, sitting forlornly at 321 Selby Street with its
rundown parking lot empty, was officially designated as a
Heritage Building by the City of Nanaimo in 1977. Too bad
they didn't designate a bit of maintenance for it at the same

Nanaimo Station — definitely down but not quite out.
Photo: Dave Preston

time, as it looked sadly disused. Its once cream-coloured walls were stained and cracked, and the blue paintwork, chipped and peeling, obviously didn't want to associate with the wood-work it had found itself on. The back of the building, where I found a desolate train platform, faces west and caught the afternoon sun. Two men were stretched out on long benches, asleep, and I wasn't sure if they were passengers or informal tenants. On a piece of coat hanger wire inside one of the windows hung an electric imitation-brass clock. Inside, some-where behind a difficult smell, the place was bleak and bare but for a couple of black benches and the washrooms, very well-used but still functioning.

A catering truck suddenly pulled onto the platform so I went outside to speak to the driver. Sandy, together with her spunky little Jack Russell terrier, Sassy, comes here twice a day, seven days a week, to meet the train. In the morning it heads north to Courtenay, and in the afternoon it heads back south to Victoria. Although it's the only food service offered on the run, business isn't lucrative. I bought a can of ice-cold orange juice and as she passed me the change I heard the loud wail of the train. The slow-moving beast, though howling to beat the band, took a while to come into view.

Sassy, who'd been quite content to hang around his owner's truck or fraternize with the customers, suddenly had his fancy taken by a black feline sitting in the parking lot across the tracks. Just as the train approached the platform he ran over the line, giving us all cause for great concern. But the train was moving at barely walking pace, giving Sandy ample time to grab the dog and bundle him through the passenger door of the truck.

A few of the passengers — about a dozen of us had assembled — bought their tickets from the guard as they boarded the single car, Dayliner No. 6135. I climbed aboard and following a garish orange carpet down the aisle, chose one of eighty equally garish red plastic seats, near the front. The car was only a quarter full at most.

We pulled away gently from Nanaimo station at 3:25 p.m. and barely made it above jogging speed for the first few miles, whistling loudly over the town's many road crossings at maybe ten miles an hour. In 1999, RailAmerica Incorporated took over the operation of the Esquimalt & Nanaimo Railway line from CP, buying the track north of here, from Nanaimo to Port Alberni, and leasing the section south of here down to Victoria. The passenger service is definitely not a moneymaker, but there are small and regular freight runs. We passed a couple of RailAmerica locomotives waiting patiently in a siding with a half-dozen boxcars for us to get by, which we eventually did. As any Vancouver Islander will tell you, things tend to move a little more slowly over here, and the train is no exception.

There's a driver's cab at both ends, so the unit is fully reversible, and the car is powered by a couple of Cummings

Passengers board the Dayliner at Nanaimo for a leisurely ride to Victoria. Photo: Dave Preston

diesel engines, each generating a scant 250 horsepower. The E & N, incidentally, was the first railway in Canada to go completely diesel when it purchased thirteen Baldwin engines in 1949. Top speed is one hundred miles per hour, though the train doesn't even reach forty miles per hour on this route. No seat-belts or white knuckles for Vancouver Island passengers.

I introduced myself to the guard, Jeff. He told me that about ten freight clients use the line, and they usually take priority over the daily passenger train and generate much more revenue. It's easy to see why this isn't a commuter run. In fact, you need a valid poetic licence to call it a run of any sort.

As we passed Nanaimo Airport, across to our left, I noticed the vehicles on the Island Highway were all travelling faster than we were. We slowed down yet again, to pass a construction crew replacing an old moss-covered bridge built in 1928 with a spanking new one in bright concrete.

A little after four o'clock we stopped in Chemainus, at Mile 51, for what was a well-practised call lasting exactly thirty seconds, during which time four people got on. This was the site of the E & N's famous robbery, when a man named Jack Adair held up the train using a wooden gun and made off (for a short while) with a $1,300 payroll.

The trackside vegetation, mainly fast-growing alders and maple, is quite dense along this narrow corridor and long-reaching views were rare. At Mile 45 we saw the first hint of coastal rain forest, cool, green and inviting with its ferns, dense cedar groves and a bubbling creek. Then we rumbled to a stop at the old Duncan station. No one got on or off, but a few people came close to the track to see what was going on and a raggle-taggle band of kids waved to us. Jeff was loathe to leave as he had a list that said people were supposed to board here, but they were nowhere in sight, so after a couple of minutes we pulled away.

We crossed a river and moved down into the pastoral Cowichan Valley, where cows grazed and farm workers pottered and summer was definitely still in attendance. I recalled being bundled up against freezing wind and drifting snow just a few days ago, and once again I realized just how big and variously beautiful is this country of ours. Just before five o'clock we passed Mile 26,

An engineer's view of the rickety E & N line, dealing with death at twenty-one miles per hour!
Photo: Dave Preston

leaving us with a marathon run to reach Victoria. I wondered if a good runner would beat us, and at the speed we were going my money would have been on the athlete.

At Mile 25 I looked out and saw a cairn made of cemented river rock. This line was completed in 1886 as the Esquimalt & Nanaimo Railway, the culmination of the national line built to unite the Canadian provinces from east to west. In 1874, the province threatened to withdraw from Confederation because the line hadn't been built as promised. To Vancouver Islanders, "...a railway to connect the seaboard of British Columbia with the railway system of Canada" meant a railway to Esquimalt, next door to Victoria, and not just to Vancouver. Their argument was strengthened by two irrefutable facts: the Island had a larger population than the B.C. mainland, and the Royal Navy had its base in Esquimalt. Prime Minister Sir John A. Macdonald encouraged Robert Dunsmuir, a local coal baron, to look into the line's feasibility and encourage its construction. It made perfect sense to Dunsmuir, who wanted rail access to the Victoria market for his Nanaimo coal, so he rounded up the same partners who helped build the Central Pacific Railway in California, and tracklaying commenced in 1885.

For once, perhaps, the government kept its word, and the prime minister used a silver hammer to drive the last spike, a golden one, into an Island railway tie on August 13, 1886. The spot is marked by the cairn at Mile 25.

The line's first passenger traffic came six weeks later, when a couple of coaches carried around fifty people from Vic West (a suburb of Victoria) to Nanaimo, at an average speed of eighteen miles per hour. Almost two years later, the E & N line was extended into burgeoning downtown Victoria.

Up until 1899, people could flag down the train at almost any point along the route and climb aboard. After dark, hunters and fishermen would light paper and wave it to catch the engineer's attention. The Island's hard-drinking coal workers often had a separate coach, known as a Miners' Local, tagged on at the back as they were apt to get a little boisterous and upset the ladies on the train. (A regular passenger on those trains was poet Robert Service, who worked for a while on a farm in Duncan.)

The E & N's seventy-eight miles of track, and a couple of steamships, were sold to the CPR in 1905 for more than $2.3 million.

Wanting to see the view from up front, I knocked on the driver's window. Five seconds later Dan introduced himself with a handshake and welcomed me into his tiny cabin. I was just in time to see the E & N line's main features, all within a couple of miles of each other. The first was a trestle we crossed, about 460 feet long and some 220 feet above the waters of Arbutus Canyon. The second was a cantilever bridge that spanned the raging Fraser River at Cisco crossing until 1912, when it was moved here to replace a wooden trestle over the Niagara River. Moments later, at Mile 15.6, we slipped through the only rock tunnel on the line, a dark little burrow of about 140 feet.

By 5:30 p.m we'd passed the dense greenery of Goldstream Park and were pulling through Langford, a suburb of Victoria, whistling merrily and stopping the rush-hour traffic at several road crossings. The rail corridor on the outskirts of town, like so many others I'd seen, was not the prettiest. Quite often, a line was built to take freight into or out of an urban area, not transport passengers. About 3 million tourists visit Victoria every year, and, fortunately for all of us, hardly any of them arrive by train. The views I saw from the E & N Dayliner as it rummaged its way through Esquimalt, passing the original Mile 0 of this line at Admirals Road, were certainly not postcard material, though several attempts had been made with a spray can of paint to brighten up the concrete scenery. However, work is underway to make this stretch of track the longest linear garden in Canada. The graffiti will be organized and sponsored, apparently, and the edges of the track are being landscaped. Much of this comes with due thanks to the Pacific Wilderness Railway, a vintage

train based in Victoria that makes several daily sightseeing runs to the Malahat Summit. Five minutes behind schedule, we pulled across the blue Johnson Street Bridge that spans the waters of Victoria's Inner Harbour. It had taken us about two and a half hours to travel 72 and a half miles from Nanaimo, an average speed of less than 30 miles per hour. A reasonably fit cyclist could have given us a good race. At 5:50 p.m. we rolled to a final halt in the diminutive station. It seemed like such a small punctuation for such a grand rail journey. But things were not always thus.

The original line ended a few hundred yards west of here, but in 1888 a swing bridge was built to carry the train across the harbour to a new station in downtown Victoria. On March 29 of that year, the first train, pulled by engine No. 4, crossed the bridge and eased its way gently through a heaving throng of five thousand people — the whole of Victoria had turned out to mark the occasion. The trans-Canadian railway had finally reached its true western terminus — British Columbia's capital city. A boisterous crowd marched in procession past decorated shops and archways to a banquet at the prestigious Driard Hotel. I had a similar march to make, but first I thanked Dan, then went and sat back down in the coach for a quiet moment with my calculator and a notebook.

My journey was over. I'd spent 106 and a half hours riding trains to get here from Halifax, and I was in no big hurry to get off. The total rail trip took almost six hours more than the VIA timetable said it should take, but there you are. According to VIA figures, I'd covered 4,387 miles by train, which, divided by those riding hours gave me an overall average speed of 41 and a half miles per hour. Not bad, considering the terrain I'd covered.

I'd been across Canada, through places with exotic names such as Miramichi, Sayabec, Saint-Hyacinthe, Gananoque, Amqui, Napanee, Gogama, Nakina and Matsqui. I'd seen the watery spots of Smith Falls, Port Hope, Clearwater, Allanwater Bridge, Savant Lake, Brereton Lake, Red Lake and Rice Lake. I'd seen Blue River, Jacquet River, Mud River and plain old Rivers, Manitoba. I'd climbed over Springhill, Mont-Joli, Montmagny, Hillsport, Sioux Lookout, Valemount, Hillbank, Cliffside and Cobble Hill. Done Sackville, Rogersville, Drummondville, Maxville, Brockville, Belleville and Melville. Tipped my hat to McKee's Camp and Strathcona Lodge. Zipped through Oba, flew past Elma, and went beyond Hope. Too bad VIA doesn't sell Trans-Canada T-shirts with all these place names.

I finally climbed down from the train and set off to keep my last appointment, with a grand old lady just around the corner — the Empress Hotel.

Victoria, the capital of British Columbia, wasn't always the genteel, tweedy maiden aunt that politely welcomes visitors seeking "a little bit of Old England." Before she adorned her lampposts with thousands of hanging flower baskets and earned the title of Garden City, she did a little time in the gut-

The Empress Hotel on Victoria's Inner Harbour — once a neighbour of the bustling CP steamship terminus, now a quiet place to sit and sip tea. Photo: Dave Preston

ter. Settled as a trading post for the Hudson's Bay Company in 1843, and named after the young Queen Victoria, the place did not attract many immigrants and seemed destined to languish as an idle outpost of the British Empire. Then a lot of miners came by, heading to the gold fields and stopping off here to buy supplies and get drunk.

For a while in the late 1850s, liquor was actually cheaper than water and bawdy houses were plentiful. The streets ran with "putrescent filth" according to the daily newpaper of the time, and people certainly didn't come here for the scenery or souvenir bottles of maple syrup. The promise of a railway, however, made a few people spring to attention, and as the CPR pushed a line across the prairies, local businessmen made sure this was "the largest and wealthiest city in the province." Not that competition was fierce.

In 1892, downtown Victoria had only one luxury hotel — the Driard (dismissing for a moment the Dallas Hotel in James Bay and the Mount Baker Hotel in Oak Bay). CP's little book, *The New Highway to the East*, describes the Driard Hotel thus:

> This hotel is so well known by all travellers to the north Pacific coast as to require but little description in these pages. Its ownership and management are not connected with the railway... the house is large and well furnished having undergone recent alterations and improvements, and it is conveniently situated near the business centre of the city.

But the Driard's days as No. 1 were numbered.

Since 1903, Captain J.W. Troup and Harry G. Barnard, two local movers and shakers, had been gathering support for a large, prestigious hotel, and they finally got the attention of the CPR. A railway bridge linking Vancouver Island to the mainland was also being promoted at the same time, so it made economic sense. The bridge was never built (although it's a perennial topic, and its building would not only be over the Strait of Georgia but over the dead bodies of many thousands of Islanders). The eager young city granted the CPR generous tax concessions and the land required — a mud flat close to the terminus of the E & N railway and the CPR steamboat dock.

The commissioned architect was Francis Mawson Rattenbury, an ambitious young man who'd left his uncle's Yorkshire firm to build a new life for himself in North America. He'd brought the French chateau style to Vancouver's Bank of Montreal building, the first major bank to establish a western operation after completion of the railroad, perhaps to remind people that it helped finance the CPR. In 1893, Rattenbury worked on Victoria's Parliament Buildings, and at the century's turn he teamed up with Samuel Maclure to build the lieutenant-governor's house here. Rattenbury's flair for exterior ideally complemented Maclure's attention to interior detail and furnishing. In 1905, Rattenbury designed the Empress Hotel.

Development of the shallow, silty bay was expensive, and foundation engineers were brought in from Boston, driving extra piles into the mud to allow for future expansion. As it rose from the ground, the Empress echoed the style of its sisters the Château Frontenac and the original Banff Springs Hotel, much as Rattenbury echoed the work of Bruce Price. His personal mark appeared in the Tudor-style arches of the front porch, the Elizabethan flavour of the lobby and the quatrefoils along the cornice (which he'd also slipped into the lieutenant-governor's residence). Much to Rattenbury's horror, the interior design was left to Mrs. Hayton Reid, wife of the CP Hotels' superintendent, who decorated and supervised the hotel furnishings.

The Empress first opened on January 21, 1908, and like its sisters suffered immediately from popularity. The original block contained 160 rooms but a north wing was added with a further 74 rooms in 1910, then a south wing with another hundred rooms in 1913. The ballroom and library, incorporated in 1912, were designed by W.S. Painter, when he wasn't tied up with his Banff Springs project.

The young Victoria was coming of age, winning the adoration of many, including the well-travelled Rudyard Kipling who said:

> To realize Victoria you must take all that the eye admires in Bournemouth, Torquay, the Isle of Wight, the happy valley at Hong Kong, the Doon, Sorrento and Camp's Bay — add reminiscences of the Thousand Islands and arrange the whole around the Bay of Naples with some Himalayas for the background.

In 1924, Rattenbury helped build the CPR Steamship Terminal, just a room key's throw from the Empress. Its massive Ionic peristyle columns remain as one of the first examples of on-site pre-cast concrete building techniques. Staring from the portals is the bearded, bewildered-looking crowned head of Poseidon — a fitting personage to marry this building with its maritime function (though it later housed a wax museum).

Hotel expansion continued; in 1929 almost three hundred more guest rooms and suites were added and the ballroom gained a conservatory. Competition for the blue-collar dollar in the late 1950s led to the city's infestation of cheap motels and motor lodges. The hotel was losing money and the manager felt he had to meet this competition head-on. So, on August 1, 1961, the

What else would one expect to find in the Bengal Room at the Empress?

Photo: The Empress Hotel

*Tea at the Empress
Hotel is sipped from
crockery exclusive to
this genteel institution.
(Putting the milk in
first is optional.)*
Photo: Dave Preston

place was rechristened the Empress Hotel and Motor Lodge, with a hundred rooms set aside in the Humboldt wing for guests who didn't need room service or someone to lug their bags. To keep costs down, piped music replaced live musicians in the dining room and commercial space was made available for rent in the lower levels.

Renovations continued over the decades, but the old lady had a major face-lift beginning in 1988, to restore some of her youthful beauty. And it was a gracefully aging dowager that received me warmly that early evening, to make the last night of my month-long journey a luxurious and memorable one.

Tweaking the schedule a little, I managed to indulge in a Victoria tradition and stepped back to an era when taking tea amid potted palms was a requisite of civilized life. In the nineteenth century, when Anna, the Duchess of Bedford, was looking to bridge the long gap between early luncheon and late evening dinner, she came up with the idea of Afternoon Tea. The refreshing hot drink was served with a few tasty sandwiches or pastries, "to combat that sinking feeling," she said. The idea caught on throughout the commonwealth, and Victoria's elderly Empress ensures that none of her guests will suffer that sinking feeling, at any cost.

The ritual of taking tea at The Empress begins with a comfortable seat in the lobby, surrounded by portraits of British monarchy. A tiered plate of delicate tea sandwiches and plump scones with homemade strawberry preserves and thick cream is graciously delivered to the table. And in a world that increasingly thinks that tea is a small stainless pot of once-hot water with a bag on the side, it is a joy to sample a properly made cup of Empress blend — China black, Ceylon and Darjeeling. Listen to the gentle strains of a Chopin waltz drifting across from the grand piano, watch the sun go down over the Inner Harbour, and complete the ritual with a refreshing selection of fresh seasonal berries. She doesn't dance on the tables or kiss you on the lips, but this dear old lady knows how to entertain a guest. The fact that the afternoon tea ritual is individually performed under this roof more than a hundred thousand times every year is a testimony to its appeal.

I finally checked in and rode the elevator up to a suite on the sixth floor. I tested the couch and all the armchairs in the living room, then tried the bed. I toured the bathroom and studied the artwork on the walls. But I was drawn back every few seconds to the windows and the view to the west, over manicured lawns and pastel-coloured rose bushes, across the waters of the harbour and up to the rolling shadows of the Sooke Hills. Perhaps it wasn't the most spectacular view I'd seen on my travels, but it was familiar to me, and it held a peace and tranquillity that none had offered before. Beyond those hills lay the world's largest ocean, so there really wasn't any farther to go by Canadian train.

I celebrated my journey's end with a fine bottle of British Columbia wine, and I toasted the Empress Hotel, and her sisters across the country in Halifax, Moncton, St. Andrews, Quebec, Montreal, Ottawa, Toronto, Winnipeg, Edmonton, Jasper, Banff, Lake Louise and Vancouver...I toasted the VIA staff, the engineers, and the people who built our country's railways...I toasted the characters I'd met along the way...I toasted Canadian scenery...I toasted Canadian food...I toasted improvised laundry techniques...and finally I raised a glass to myself for having made the trip and not missed a single train nor lost a single room key.

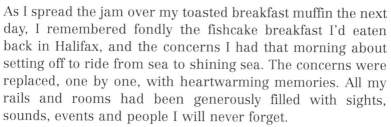

As I spread the jam over my toasted breakfast muffin the next day, I remembered fondly the fishcake breakfast I'd eaten back in Halifax, and the concerns I had that morning about setting off to ride from sea to shining sea. The concerns were replaced, one by one, with heartwarming memories. All my rails and rooms had been generously filled with sights, sounds, events and people I will never forget.

I checked out of the Empress and walked purposefully across the street, then down a few stone steps to the causeway of the Inner Harbour. I walked to the end of the wooden dock, knelt down and reached into my shirt pocket for the small canister of Atlantic seawater. I flipped the top, and with a silent prayer that I'd once again see Halifax Harbour, I let the contents spill into the dark water below me. All I had left to do now was find my way home.

A drop of Atlantic Ocean, scooped from Halifax Harbour, finds a new home the Pacific after a journey of 5,225 miles.

Photo: Lesley Preston

Index